The Field Guide to Guide to Bigfoot, Yeti, and Other Mystery Primates Worldwide

Other FIELD GUIDES
from Avon Books

THE FIELD GUIDE TO EXTRATERRESTRIALS
by Patrick Huyghe
Illustrated by Harry Trumbore

The Field Guide to Bigfoot, Yeti, and Other Mystery Primates Worldwide

LOREN COLEMAN and PATRICK HUYGHE

Illustrated by Harry Trumbore

AVON BOOKS ◥◣ NEW YORK

AVON BOOKS, INC.
1350 Avenue of the Americas
New York, New York 10019

Library of Congress Cataloging in Publication Data:

Coleman, Loren.
    The field guide to Bigfoot, Yeti, and other mystery primates
    worldwide / by Loren Coleman and Patrick Huyghe : illustrated by
    Harry Trumbore.
        p. cm.
    Includes bibliographical references (p.   ) and index.
    1. Monsters. 2. Primates—Folklore. I. Huyghe, Patrick.
    II. Title.
    QL89.C645 1999   99-11792
    001.944—dc21   CIP

First Avon Books Trade Paperback Printing: April 1999

AVON TRADEMARK REG. U.S. PAT. OFF. AND IN OTHER COUNTRIES,
MARCA REGISTRADA, HECHO EN U.S.A.

Printed in the U.S.A.

OPM   10 9 8 7 6 5 4 3 2 1

For Malcolm, Caleb, Desmond
. . . and Alexandra

All great truths begin as blasphemies.
—George Bernard Shaw

CONTENTS

The Field Guide to Bigfoot, Yeti, and Other Mystery Primates Worldwide

INTRODUCTION

A FAMILY MATTER

We are not alone. If there is any truth to the testimony of eyewitnesses worldwide, we appear to live amid a variety of humanlike and apelike creatures whose existence has been largely ignored, forgotten, or denied, at least in recent history. Despite the crowding of the earth's surface with our species and the encroachment of *Homo sapiens* into the mountains, wildernesses, and wild places around the world, there is apparently ample room left over for our elusive cousins to hide. And they have done just that—for the most part. But as the reports of encounters accumulate, it has become increasingly clear that an understanding of these creatures lies not in myth, folklore, and legend, but, ultimately, in reality.

Now, as the twentieth century draws to a close, we respectfully suggest that the time has come to explore, without prejudice, the possibility that we are sharing this planet with an assortment of near-human beings, distant relatives who have not been invited into the parlor but who surely must be in the family tree. The vast populations of "Bigfoot," the generic name that the media and the public have bestowed upon hairy hominoids—the humans, apes, and other primates you will read about in this book—appear to be widespread, of many different types, and neighbors of a sort.

There is surely more to the story of human evolution than mainstream anthropology has presented to us to date, discomforting though that thought may be. It's one thing to realize, as scientists and popular writers have made clear, that we are the "naked ape" or the "third chimpanzee." It's still another shocking step to grasp the notion that in the not too distant past modern humans shared the earth with other humanlike creatures known as hominids. But who is ready to accept the idea that some close cousins still live with us on this planet today, though largely without our knowledge? Something is happening here, and our realization of it is sure to be revolutionary.

Just as Linnaeus, in 1735, envisioned bringing order to the chaos that reigned between cultures, nations, languages, and different authors with regard to life-forms in the natural world, we hope this field guide brings some order to the mass of reports of seemingly unrelated and diverse species of unknown hairy hominoids seen worldwide. Following standard anthropological, zoological, and paleoanthropological parameters of identification, our field guide attempts to systematically classify those unknown hairy hominoids who appear to inhabit this globe. Certainly, the process of analyzing the data—the traditions, sightings, footprint finds, behaviors, range patterns, and more—has led us to a greater understanding of the overall diversity and linkages among these apparent earthmates of ours. We were surprised, and no doubt you will be, too.

ALL TOGETHER NOW

The existence of some creatures in this book is more controversial than others. New apes and monkeys, even large ones, are one thing; new hominids are something else entirely. Most people believe that *Homo sapiens* ("A Wise Man") are the only hominids alive today. But are we? The same logic that supports this belief has also been thought to hold true of hominids in the past. But scientists now realize that the notion of only one hominid species living at any one time throughout human evolution is clearly wrong. For decades anthropologists had held firmly to a rule of thumb called the Single Species Hypothesis when looking for our fossil ancestors. That hypothesis essentially states that only one species of a particular kind can inhabit a specific ecological niche at any given time because of competition for food and other resources. But over the past twenty years that view has steadily crumbled.

The Single Species Hypothesis simply does not hold for Africa. In 1975, a nearly complete skull of an ancient early human, since named *Homo ergaster,* was unearthed from the same two-million-year-old sediment at Olduvai Gorge, Tanzania, that six years earlier had revealed a nearly complete skull of the tall, robust, primitive, crested apeman *Paranthropus boisei* (also called *Australapithecus boisei*). These and later findings, including some from South Africa, suggest that less than 2 million years ago, there were actually six species of hominids coexisting in southern and eastern Africa; three were different species of the large, robust apemen *Paranthropus,* and three were species of early humans, *Homo* (*habilis, rudolfensis,* and *ergaster*).

The same situation—this coexistence of hominids—apparently held true in Asia, but, notably, much more recently. In Southeast Asia, during the 1940s, the paleoanthropologists Franz Weidenreich and Ralph von Koenigswald found evidence, generally ignored by anthropologists, that *Gigantopithecus* (a very strong and enormous anthropoid ape), *Meganthropus palaeojavanicus* (great man of ancient Java, known today as *Paranthropus*), and two different species or subspecies of *Homo erectus* (namely the Java apeman and the Peking man), all lived at the same time. Then in 1996, Carl C. Swisher III of the Berkeley Geochronology Center found new data indicating that *Homo erectus* had indeed lived in Java at the same time as *Homo sapiens,* the modern human. Using new techniques to date fossils found at Solo River, Java, Swisher's team concluded that the supposedly very much older species known as *Homo erectus* had actually lived in Java as recently as 53,000 to 27,000 years ago. This was earthshaking news to anthropologists who had assumed a much more ancient date for *erectus.*

Also in 1996, researchers led by Russell Ciochon and Vu The Long discussed the apparent coexistence of *Homo erectus* and *Gigantopithecus blacki* in Tham Khuyen Cave, Vietnam. This giant ape was contemporaneous with archaic humans throughout its range from 6 million to 300,000 years ago. That is quite a long and successful span of coexistence, and *Gigantopithecus* must have been a formidable "neighbor"—a true giant on the landscape of the world with the little near-humans and humans like so many troublesome distant cousins breeding furiously and taking up living space.

The situation in Europe was no different. It is rather well established now that Neandertal man (*Homo neanderthalensis*) were not our ancestors, but a side branch that may have already been living in Europe when the first modern humans (*Homo sapiens*) arrived. From fossil finds at Mt. Carmel in Israel, we know the two species coexisted for more than 50,000 years. And recent finds at Zafarraya in Spain suggest that Neandertals may have survived longer than previously thought, living perhaps as recently as 27,000 years ago, long after modern humans had set up residence.

Clearly our ancestors coexisted with many types and kinds of fossil humans, near-men, fossil apes, modern apes, and modern humans. They all lived at the same time. Surprising findings and new evidence continue to reinforce the fact that we have rarely been alone—and may not be today. Other hairy hominoids may still be our neighbors, perhaps well hidden, but our contemporaries nonetheless.

THE LUMPING PROBLEM

What is a "Bigfoot"? Therein lies a grand tale of a great tradition that stretches back . . . only forty years! Today when people talk about stories of monsters in the woods, wildmen in the forests, giants on the tundra, hairy bipeds in the suburbs, and apes in the swamps, whether in Maryland or Malaysia, California or China, the word used in the popular media and in the public mind is "Bigfoot."

Before "Bigfoot" came along as a handy tag for strange reports of hairy creatures in every corner of the world, the 1950s label was "Abominable Snowman" or "Yeti." And before that, during the last century, the phrase was "Wildman," with a few examples of newspapers using "apeman" or "caveman" as well. This was true throughout the English-speaking and Western world.

"Bigfoot," of course, is the name given to those unknown hairy hominids with large humanlike footprints and an upright stance who are found in the Pacific Northwest of the United

States. But it was not always so, even in North America. The Canadian version of Bigfoot, called "Sasquatch," has an even longer history. Prior to the 1950s, most media attention regarding hairy hominoid reports in the Pacific Northwest was limited to a few minor stories on Canada's "Sasquatch." According to researchers John Green and Ivan T. Sanderson, this Indian-sounding word was first coined in the 1920s by J. W. Burns, a teacher who for years collected wild, hairy giant stories from his Chehalis Indian friends. Burns combined several similar Native Canadians' names for these creatures and created the word "Sasquatch." In recent years, scientists and folklorists looking to bring respectability to the subject have been using the more scholarly-sounding term "Sasquatch." But most people coast to coast and around the world still call these creatures "Bigfoot."

The first use of the label "Bigfoot," now so widely disseminated by the media, did not occur until a credible, churchgoing bulldozer operator named Jerry Crew appeared at a northern California newspaper office with the plaster cast of one of many large hominid footprints he had found in the mud in Bluff Creek Valley. His widely reprinted account—and photograph holding the cast, which stretches from his collar to his belt—first appeared in the *Humboldt Times,* along with the word "Bigfoot," on October 5, 1958. The story was written by the paper's "RFD" columnist and editor Andrew Genzoli, who deserves credit for bringing the word "Bigfoot," as the road construction workers were calling this big-footed creature, to the outside world.

The naming of Bigfoot was a significant cultural event. To deny this would be to ignore how intrinsic Bigfoot has become in global day-to-day living, reflected in products from a special type of pizza to snow skis to characters in international films, as well as scores of other commercial examples. Today most grade school children anywhere in the world can talk with authority about Bigfoot and draw a picture of what they think it looks like.

This widespread use of the term "Bigfoot" has been, in one sense, quite beneficial. Before reports of Bigfoot were so routinely published in the press, there was scant recognition of the widespread nature of the sightings and folklore about unknown hominoids, shaggy forest giants, and swamp apes. But since the advent of "Bigfoot," this word has actually made it easier for law enforcement officers, media reporters, and the general public to accept and "file" sightings of all kinds of unknown hairy hominoids. A report of a 7-foot-tall, brown-haired, white-maned creature seen in Ohio might have been ignored in 1941, but in 1971, it was duly collected and written up as an "out-of-place Bigfoot." Such is the affirmative nature of the name.

But the enormous popularity of "Bigfoot" has also been a tremendous drawback to research into the subject. "Bigfoot" has become such an easy, silly-sounding handle for any wild, hairy upright being, that is it used almost universally by writers—and naturally avoided by most anthropologists. The use of "Bigfoot"—as well as a few other regional favorite names like "Yowie," "Yeti," "Yeren," "Wildman," and "Snowman"—has clouded the distinctive names that are often employed by locals and native peoples to describe their wildlife. There seem to be three or four animals being called "Yeti" in the Himalayas, maybe three named "Yeren" in China, and so forth, but there are literally hundreds of local types and perhaps as many as eight large kinds or classes of animals termed "Bigfoot." Just as the Inuit (Eskimo) are said to have at least fifteen different "words" (actually, lexemes which can be thought of as independent vocabulary items or dictionary entries) for the English concept "snow," so too do native peoples often have several words or phrases for different kinds of animals that to outsiders are merely "wild ones," "ape-people," "monkeys," or "apes."

The concept of Bigfoot, in other words, hides a larger truth, lumps considerable differences and just plain confuses the picture. In our global natural history culture, "Bigfoot" throws into a blender any notion of the many differences in behavior, footprints, hair color, height, physique, family units, diet, living arrangements, daily cycle, and other unique overall patterns that exist from one group of these beings to another. This field guide addresses this problem by looking at the great diversity in reports and how they naturally group into zoologically logical collections of similar animals. We have created a classification system that delivers thoughtful, biologically-based groupings for the great number of different kinds of unknown primates that are apparently out there. Of course, we were not the first to do so.

ABOMINABLE ROSTERS

We saw the beginnings of our species's need to catalog when early humans first began to collect in families and discuss totem clans to which they belonged. And then, when the study of the natural order of things was formalized, humans organized the animals, including the anthropoids and hominoids, into their own "families"—whether they be called "genus" or "order" or "class." This exercise assists our understanding of relationships in the world and we tend to feel more comfortable with the end results of such undertakings. The study of as yet undiscovered, usually hairy, hominids (hominology) and primates of concern to cryptozoology (the study of animals as yet unrecognized by science) is no different.

Thousands of years of human interactions with these creatures have led to centuries of attempts to chronicle the encounters between "us" and "them." At first, writers merely recorded the sightings as part of their attempts to capture what was unknown and on the edge of biology. Travelogues did this, and early accounts by government officials, explorers, and naturalists continued the tradition of "traveler's tales" of the curious new wildlife they had seen. Recording stories and sightings of hairy hominoids was viewed as simply putting down on paper what any good observer would see going into a "new land." All things seemed possible, and the well-educated journalist (in its original meaning, one who writes as one journeys) would naturally record the firsthand encounters and secondhand tales of giants, hairy men, and little people. With the age of enlightenment, reason ruled and it was declared time to address the confusion that reigned in the new sciences. Linnaeus's classification system would then become the apex achievement of this ordering of the natural universe.

But how would these near-humans be dealt with in the new

world order? Apes were one thing, but hairy manlike beasts were another. Many quickly got the boot into the world of myth and lore, a "Goblin Universe" that some later writers have noted was developed to wrestle with the question of too many beings inhabiting the Earth. Classification systems were created for these denizens that could only have space reserved for them in the netherland of legend. As the anthropologist John Napier points out, this kind of sorting became so detailed that classical Greek mythology, for example, recognized three types of Cyclopes.

But what of the "real" biological world? What of those who recognized some biological basis for the continuing reports of hairy hominoids that seemed not quite human? Actually Linnaeus (born Karl von Linne), the Swedish naturalist and founder of systematic nomenclature, began it all in 1735 when he found a place in the classification system for some of these creatures. Linnaeus took the travelers' reports of Wildmen to be true, for example, and named them variously *Homo nocturnus* (the man of the night), *Homo troglodytes* (cave man), and *Homo ferus* (wild man). But two hundred years would pass before we could revisit the classification of such creatures. The Linnaean revolution was slow in catching up to Bigfoot.

Decades of authors writing about Wildmen and Snowmen— some in the nineteenth century, like John Ashton, Francis Buckland, and Charles Gould, and an increasing number, mostly in the mid-twentieth century, including Willy Ley, Herbert Wendt, and the "Father of Cryptozoology" himself, Bernard Heuvelmans—never systematically organized their data, that is, the eyewitness reports, the physical evidence, the footprints, and the folklore of these animals, into categories of hominoid classifications. This seems to have occurred for several reasons, but most frequently it happened because these authors wrote of a series of incidents in one geographical area separate from others elsewhere. For example, Wendt discussed Abominable Snowmen, South American apes, Satyrs, and hairy Wild People, but never placed them in any overall framework of hominoids, discovered and undiscovered. Ley wrote of Himalayan Yetis in isolation from all other reports around the world, while, on the other hand, trying to relate several different kinds of proto-pygmy reports and theories to a more global examination of the Little People. Efforts were spotty. Heuvelmans, of course, tackled many more topics than anyone before him. Though his early works were comprehensive *within the individual treatment of each creature,* he did not classify them or systematically link one to another. Even Heuvelmans's very noteworthy 1986 "Checklist of Apparently Unknown Animals" is just that, a checklist, not a classification system, and he never claimed it was anything more.

But with one major work, this centuries-long oversight would end. With the publication in 1961 of Ivan T. Sanderson's omnibus volume, *Abominable Snowmen: Legend Come to Life,* the study of hominoids found its Linneaus. A man who had led zoological collection expeditions into the rain forests of Africa and South America, a biologist with a degree from Cambridge, a Scotsman living in America, Sanderson was the perfect choice to categorize what he called the ABSMs ("Abominable Snowmen") of the world. Having gathered reports from around the globe for decades before his book came out, Sanderson had always been on the leading edge of discoveries, which he popularized in his magazine articles, books, and television appearances on controversial subjects.

While others had simply looked regionally to discuss their hairy hominoids, Sanderson took a comprehensive global look at the reports and other evidence. Sanderson found that the individual names of these ABSMs numbered in the hundreds from people to people, tribe to tribe, but he noticed an underlying oneness and natural groupings. "We should understand the number of names for ABSMs has nothing to do with the number of different kinds of these creatures," he wrote. "There are literally hundreds of names for ABSMs still in use today, and hundreds more in over half the languages on earth and in many more that have now passed into common usage." But Sanderson also realized that while some ABSMs have wide distributions, others have very restricted ones, and that the size of a creature did not matter greatly since regional and individual variations would come into play within a type.

Ivan T. Sanderson grounded his classification system, and indeed his entire body of work, in the geography of vegetation—"desert, scrublands, savannahs and prairies, orchard and parklands, woods and forests, and most especially of montane forests on uplands and mountains." In other words, similar creatures tend to inhabit similar environments. Beyond that Sanderson tried to distinguish between the "manlike" and the "apelike" creatures. So it was that Sanderson created a classification system that began with the "most manlike" creatures, what he called the "Sub-Humans," followed by the "Proto-Pigmies" and the "Neo-Giants," and ending with the "least manlike," but not necessarily "more apelike," "Sub-Hominids."

Some researchers applauded Sanderson's efforts. The anthropologist John Napier was impressed, calling it "an eye-opener for anyone who imagines that the Yeti of the Himalayas is the only manifestation of the genre. . . . It rather makes the mind boggle that there should be a whole *Systema Naturae* of unknown, living monsters. . . ." But others, who preferred to lump such creatures together rather than distinguish between them as Sanderson had done, were not so kind. Grover S. Krantz, the University of Washington anthropologist, did not see "any compelling evidence for more than one type of hairy biped" and found "no reason to think it has anywhere near worldwide distribution." Krantz believes Bigfoot is linked to *Gigantopithecus* and occurs over most of North America and northern Asia "and that is all."

Two decades after Sanderson, the British anthropologist Myra Shackley surveyed the situation in her book *Still Living?* and divided the reports of hairy hominids worldwide into just three types: (1) the *chuchunaa* from Siberia, which she theorized were now extinct or assimilated by humans; (2) the Sasquatch or Yeti (she used the terms interchangeably), which are present in North America, the Himalayas, the Pamirs, Siberia, and China, and which she linked to *Gigantopithecus;* and (3) the *almas,* which range from the Caucasus Mountains eastward to Mongolia, and which Shackley believes are probably Neandertals. Due to her own research in Neandertal paleoarchaeology, Shackley's main focus was equating the *almas* to the Neandertals. But critiques of her work point out that she used outdated models of subhuman Neandertals for comparing the very subhuman, not-so-bright *almas* with what we now know to be the very different but intelligent and physically humanlike Neandertals.

Since the early 1960s two other researchers began elaborating on and extending Sanderson's typology, as new sighting reports, new footprint finds, and new fossil evidence became available. One of these researchers was Loren Coleman. He was one of the first to notice the widespread distribution of three or more different kinds of hairy bipedal creatures in eastern North America and distinguished them from those in the Pacific Northwest. His most significant contribution during the 1960s was his development of a theory concerning "North American Apes," which he called Napes. He theorized that evidence of footprints and sightings demonstrated that a dryopithecine-like, chimpanzee-like ape that is *not* Bigfoot was extant throughout the American South and Midwest temperate and subtropical hardwood forests.

In 1970 Coleman and hominoid researcher Mark A. Hall collaborated on a milestone paper that uncovered strong Native American, Native Canadian, and Inuit traditions across North America in support of creatures generally labeled "Bigfoot" in modern times. By the 1980s, Coleman, along with Hall and anomalist David Fideler, had gathered dozens of reports of so-called American kangaroos and their three-toed tracks and theorized, along with Hall, that these were an aberrant form of giant monkey. Most recently, Coleman, again working with Hall's data, discovered the piebald, or two-tone, nature of a group of hominids reported throughout subarctic and nearby colder regions of the world. These he calls the "Marked Hominids."

Like Coleman, Hall has thought deeply about classifications over the past three decades. In a volume entitled *The Yeti, Bigfoot & True Giants,* revised in 1997 but based on writings dating back more than a quarter century, Hall proposed a sixfold classification system based on four categories of evidence that identify the different types of primates—the unique characteristics and width-to-length ratio of the tracks reportedly left behind by these creatures, the creatures' modern physical descriptions, the long-extant traditions that match the modern physical descriptions, and the fossil finds that agree with what is described as being alive today.

Hall's first group is the "Neo-Giants." While this is the same name that Sanderson used for these creatures, Hall restricts its use to the reports of somewhat shorter hairy giants, namely those up to 9 feet in height. These creatures leave hourglass-shaped tracks up to 20 inches in length, have a split ball, and have similar-sized toes with an oblique slant. Then out from Sanderson's Neo-Giants, Hall split off the "True Giants," for those truly tall giants that are routinely over 10 feet tall and leave behind huge four-toed tracks. Hall calls his third class "Yetis," which includes not only the man-sized, rocking-climbing, unknown apes seen only in the Himalayas but also all of the 5- to 6-foot-tall pongids (apes) seen around the world who leave behind very distinctive apelike tracks about a foot long with the big toe sticking out to the side. Hall's fourth class is the "Taller-Hominids," who are up to 7 feet tall. Their narrow feet leave a curving impression that measures up to 14.5 inches long and display toes that are splayed.

Hall's "Shorter-Hominids," his fifth class, are moderate-sized hairy Neandertaloids who leave tracks that measure up to 15 inches. Their toes are similar in shape and spread apart, with the big toe clearly angled away from the others. The "Little People" are Hall's sixth class. They are always under 5 feet in height and leave tiny footprints with distinctive toes and pointed heels that are not at all like those of human children. Then, in 1997, Hall split off a distinct group of creatures from his Shorter-Hominids and created a seventh class of creatures which he calls the "Least Hominids." These represent the less intelligent, more primitive, but also rare (therefore "Least") *Homo erectus,* separated from the behaviorally and descriptively different Neandertaloids left in the category "Shorter-Hominids."

A NEW CLASSIFICATION SYSTEM

We recognize that "it would be easiest to sell the existence of 'Bigfoot' to the public and to science if there were only one type of creature yet unrecognized," as Mark A. Hall has noted. But reality demands otherwise. Nature has never been known for its simplicity.

In producing this field guide, we have reviewed all past efforts at classifying the world's mystery primates and developed a new nine-part system that, while relying heavily on the work of others, manages to introduce some new concepts that we feel best encompasses all the evidence available to date. We essentially accept Hall's revision of Sanderson's Neo-Giant, as well as Hall's new True Giant classifications. But what Hall called the Taller-Hominid we have renamed "Marked Hominids" because we wished to avoid yet another classification name that seemed to hinge solely on the creature's height. We also have a more restricted view of its range than Hall. And for what Hall calls the Little People we have picked a name that harks back to a variant of Sanderson's Proto-Pigmies, our "Proto-Pygmies." We feel that the term "Little People" is too closely related to one type of folklore entity. Our "Unknown Pongid" class combines the more "bestial" members of Sanderson's Sub-Hominids type with members of Hall's Yeti group, a name that we feel is too closely linked to creatures of the Himalayas. Our Unknown Pongid class is therefore not encumbered with the old baggage that accompanies the Yeti name or tied to a region, but instead expands the category to include truly unknown pongids worldwide. Hall's Shorter-Hominids and his new branch off from that group, the Least-Hominids, rather closely match our "Neandertaloid" and "Erectus Hominid" classes, but we feel that these names are more descriptive of the kinds of creatures being seen. Sanderson's Sub-Humans contained hominids that now are mainly listed in our Neandertaloid and Erectus Hominid classes.

Two classes are entirely new with this classification system, privately discussed between Coleman and Hall but little publicized. We have a class for "Giant Monkeys" to describe those creatures that appear to be a rather important group of giant baboonlike primates. And we have chosen to describe a type of primate that apparently lives in sea and freshwater systems as "Merbeings." This group may be the least known to hominologists, because most researchers have not looked at the accounts of Mermaids, Lizardmen, and *chupacabras* as perhaps representing new, undiscovered primates. While we may be ridiculed for such a bold class that seems to involve creatures of myth and legend, we have based this class, like the others, on a careful examination of solid evidence of a biological basis.

A complete description of each of our nine classes follows, accompanied by a worldwide distribution map for each class. These maps take a wide range of material into account—footprint finds, physical evidence, and eyewitness sightings, of course, but also native traditions, native art, old news accounts, as well as folklore and legend.

1.
NEO-GIANT

 Neo-Giants are unique animals found in the mountain forests of the Pacific Rim, specifically the American and Canadian Pacific Northwest, the western parts of Central and South America, as well as southern China, Tibet, and Indochina. They are known locally by such names as Bigfoot, Sasquatch, *oh-mah*, *sisemite*, *ucumar*, and *gin-sung*.

The Neo-Giant ranges in height from 6 to 9 feet at maturity. They have stocky bodies, with enormous barrel torsos and clearly visible large breasts on older females. Their heads are small and pointed with no visible neck or forehead and they have a heavy browridge that sports a continuous upcurled fringe of hair. The faces of the young are generally light colored while those of older individuals tend to be dark. Their jaws project forward markedly and their eyes are small, round, and dark.

The hair of the Neo-Giant tends to be shaggy and relatively short but shows no difference in length between body and head hair. In the young the hair is usually dark; it moves into shades of red and brown with age and finally, at extreme maturity, evidences some silver. Overall the shape of the Neo-Giant foot has an hourglass outline and measures 4 to 9 inches in width by 11.75 to 20 inches in length. But halfway down the foot's contour is a "split-ball" or double ball arrangement that is character-

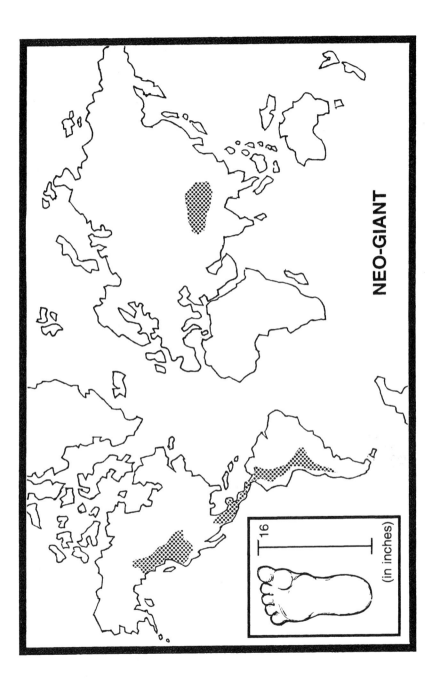

NEO-GIANT

16

(in inches)

istic of this class. Each foot shows five toes with some possible webbing at the base of the last joints.

Neo-Giants are nocturnal. They are retiring, alert, and wily, generally avoiding humans, though firsthand encounters and native folklore indicate they have a tendency to kidnap females and some males. They don't wear clothes of any kind and never display weapons or tools. They seem to nest in caves or beds made in the open and in trees. They appear to be vegetarian, though they have been seen to take pikas, other small rodents, and fish on occasion. Neo-Giants are highly vocal, making high-pitched whistles, animal-like screams, howls, and such sounds as "eeek-eeek-eeek," "sooka-sooka-sooka," "ugh-ugh-ugh," and "uhu-uhu-uhu."

Various scientific names have been proposed for Bigfoot and the other animals we call Neo-Giants. In the 1960s, the primatologist W. C. Osman Hill suggested that Bigfoot be named *Nearctic chionanthropus*. But Grover Krantz, an anthropologist from the University of Washington, favors *Gigantopithecus blacki,* based on footprint evidence alone. A different species of this genus would have Krantz naming it *Gigantopithecus canadensis,* as *canadensis* is a frequently used zoological name for native species of northern North America. If Bigfoot are an entirely new genus, Krantz would name it *Gigantoanthropus*.

The other widely favored fossil affinity for Bigfoot was proposed in 1971 by Gordon Strasenburgh, a political scientist with an interest in Bigfoot. He thought Bigfoot would be found to be related to *Paranthropus robustus* and suggested that the name *Paranthropus eldurrelli* be used for the Bigfoot of the Pacific Northwest. *Paranthropus* is a fossil hominid genus initially assigned by paleontologist Robert Broom to a robust form of australopithecine found at Kromdraai and Swartkrans in South Africa. One of the most famous *Paranthropus* species is *boisei,* discovered by Mary Leakey in 1959 at Olduvai Gorge in Tanzania. It is known for its massive jaw muscles and huge back teeth the size of quarters that inspired the nickname "Nutcracker Man." But if these hominids are Bigfoot, Krantz favors the name *Australopithecus robustus* instead, or *Australopithecus canadensis* if Bigfoot is a new robust species of the genus *Australopithecus.* (The term *Australopithecus robustus* was used for *Paranthropus* by some anthropologists during the 1970s and 1980s.)

The evidence gathered to date suggests the Neo-Giants could very well be *Paranthropus* (while the True Giants, the next class described, maintain a greater affinity to *Gigantopithecus*). In Neo-Giants, as in primates that have large jaws and well-developed chewing muscles (e.g., gorillas and baboons), the skull's parietal bone continues upward at the midline to form a sagittal crest. The early hominid fossil evidence shows that *Paranthropus* of both genders exhibited a sagittal crest—a feature that provides a very strong link to the male and female Neo-Giants seen today.

2.
TRUE GIANT

If there were ever giants on this Earth, they existed long, long ago. Or so goes prevailing opinion on the subject. But by the late 1960s, some researchers began to realize that something bigger than Bigfoot was out there being seen and leaving enormous tracks nearly 2 feet long. One of these researchers, the Canadian John Green, had noticed from the accounts he had collected in North America that a whole group of "giants" existed who were clearly bigger than the Sasquatch of the Pacific Northwest. Green was convinced that the evidence supported their existence, because he had talked to the witnesses who were very certain as to what they had seen. But it was researcher Mark A. Hall who first gave this group of creatures the name "True Giants." Hall had spent years examining the growing body of data pointing to this distinctive group of extremely large hairy hominids who routinely left long, four-toed footprints.

For creatures said to be 10 to 20 feet tall, the term "True

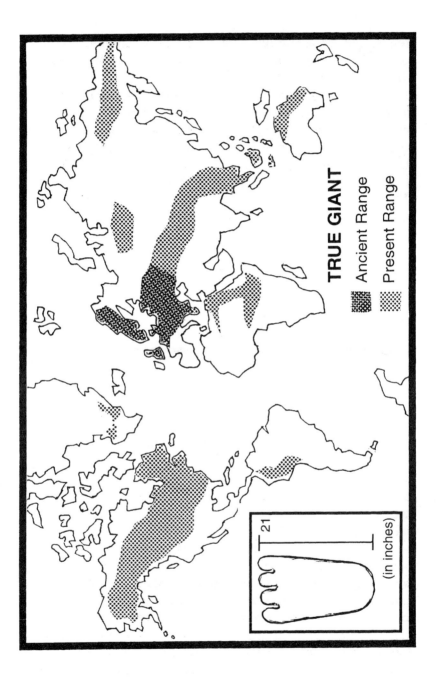

TRUE GIANT

Ancient Range

Present Range

21

(in inches)

Giants" is most appropriate. The big bodies of True Giants are remarkably lean, if not lanky, and are covered with reddish brown or darker hair that is longer on the head and thinner on the arms. They appear to have no neck and their facial features are flat. They have enormous, flat hands. Their feet measure about 10 inches wide by 21 inches long or longer, and they have four visible toes; if they have a fifth vestigial toe, it does not show up in most prints.

True Giants are reported in wooded mountain areas around the world, mostly in temperate zones, and are known by such popular names as *gilyuk, misabe, chenoo, nyalmo, orang dalam,* and *ferla mohr.* A large body of international folktales recounts the interactions, communication, warfare, and eventually estrangement between native peoples and True Giants. Though they are said to be omnivorous and have a reputation as man eaters (the cannibals of bygone days), they have tended to avoid confrontations with humans in recent times.

True Giants occasionally wear primitive clothing, especially in colder climates, and they often sport wooden clubs or stone weapons. Reports suggest that they live in caves with concealed entrances and sleep in depressions they make in the ground. While basically nocturnal, these creatures are occasionally seen during the day if there is enough tree cover to keep them hidden from most observers. The movements of True Giants tend to look wobbly to observers, who sometimes report sounds coming from these creatures, perhaps a primitive form of language.

Researcher Mark A. Hall links True Giants to the fossil form known as *Gigantopithecus.* Giganto, as the species is popularly called, appears to be the largest primate to have ever existed. Though Giganto is thought to have existed for more than 5.5 million years, the only traces we have of it are four enormous jawbones and a thousand fossil teeth found in China, Vietnam, and India. Giganto was one of the most successful primates ever, living side by side with several different species of *Homo* for millions of years until it disappeared from the fossil record a mere 500,000 to 300,000 years before the present. In reconstructions, *Gigantopithecus* is usually portrayed as a super-gorilla shown on all fours on the ground. But more recently, some scientists have shown it as an upright primate, reaching a height of about 10 feet. Based on True Giant eyewitness accounts, Hall attributes a bipedal stance and much taller heights to *Gigantopithecus*.

3.
MARKED HOMINID

One remarkable feature seems to set apart a group of 7-foot-tall hairy hominids usually seen in and near the subpolar regions of the world. In this population, the individuals tend to be piebald—exhibiting either a two-toned, multicolored hair pattern; a lighter-haired mane; a near-albino appearance; or a white patch in the midst of a field of darker hair. The Siberians called one such individual Mecheny, meaning the Marked One, and since that seems a fitting name, we have decided to call this entire class the Marked Hominids. This name serves the double purpose of being a fitting tribute to the man who discovered the uniqueness in the tracks and descriptions of the Marked Hominids, Mark A. Hall.

Though often mistaken for Sasquatch, Marked Hominids are actually more human-looking and somewhat shorter than the classic Neo-Giant. They average about seven feet tall and have firm, powerful bodies with well-developed legs and shoulder muscles. Their arms do not reach below the knees, they have flat buttocks, visible genitalia, and sometimes a protruding stomach, which is probably indicative of the individual's age and well-fed condition. Also characteristic is a foot that measures 10 to 14.5 inches long, has a narrow curving impression, and a 3 to 5 inch width. Its five toes are splayed; often even the outside, or little, toe appears splayed.

The Marked Hominid is essentially neckless and has large eyes

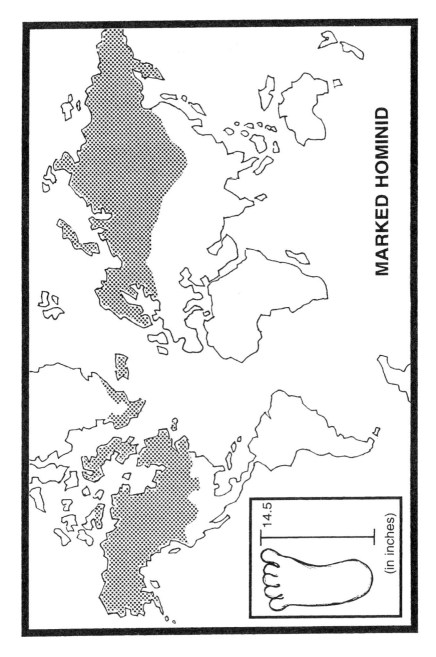

MARKED HOMINID

14.5

(in inches)

set in a rounded face with a calm, almost pleasant, appearance. They do not look apelike at all. In males, the face has hair, or a beard, from the eyes down, so that it looks like they are wearing a mask. Their hair is short, brown or black, and slightly longer on the head, under the arms, and in the pubic area. As noted, they have a tendency to be piebald, showing lighter patches among the darker colors, but can be albino or light maned.

Though the Marked Hominid may exist globally, it appears to live mainly on the wooded mountainsides and tundra in the subpolar regions of North America, Europe, and Asia. This howling nocturnal creature sometimes wears skins and often smells like a wet dog. Though they may live in groups, the Marked Hominids do not appear to be as intelligent as the native peoples with whom they have shared similar harsh living conditions. The Marked Hominids have been known to approach human housing and livestock, trade with humans, and communicate with them nonverbally. A byproduct of their close association with humans is their natural annoyance with dogs, which, according to reports, they have sometimes killed.

The diet of the Marked Hominid shows a preference for larger mammals, small game, and plants. In April 1992, Vyacheslav Oparin, a Karelian journalist, was promoting the idea that Finland's Abominable Snowman should be renamed the Forest Monster or Tree Eater because, he claimed, the tall and hairy animals living along the Finnish border climbed trees and lived off bark.

A fossil affinity for the Marked Hominids has only recently been discovered. In 1929, anthropologist F. C. C. Hansen published a description of a massive skull including the mandible found in a 1926 archeological dig near the former site of Gardar, Greenland. Hansen related it to the finds of ancient skulls, such as the Rhodesian man, and named the species *Homo gardarensis.* Mark A. Hall rediscovered this information in the mid-1990s, bringing to our attention the finds from Greenland and his discovery of their connection to reports of a unique kind of unknown hairy hominid. (*Homo gardarensis* may, in fact, be a recent form of the giant European fossil man, *Homo heidelbergensis.*) According to Hall, the fossil finds which anthropologists have labeled *Homo gardarensis* fit perfectly the tales of the *tornit* told by the Inuit (Eskimo), the *chuchunaa* described by the people of Siberia, and the Marked Hominids still seen today.

4.
NEANDERTALOID

Thanks to a number of best-selling novels and Hollywood movies, Neandertals are enjoying a high profile in popular culture these days. No doubt part of the attraction comes from the underlying notion—long suggested by such researchers as Ivan T. Sanderson, John Pfeiffer, Myra Shackley, Dimitri Bayanov, Igor Bourtsev, Boris Porshnev, and Bernard Heuvelmans—that relict populations of Neandertals may still be roaming Asia and parts of the rest of the world, leaving classic Neandertal tracks and being seen as some kind of hairy Wildmen. But a reanalysis of the contemporary accounts that some claim to be of Neandertal origin suggests that most are not Neandertals at all. According to Mark Hall, they are more likely to be Erectus Hominids, our next class, instead.

Neandertaloids are one of the most infrequently seen of the nine classes in this field guide, either because they manage to stay so well hidden from *Homo sapiens* or because they are so few in number. Their large footprints are rarely found, but when they are, the dramatic tracks tend to attract a good deal of publicity. Modern sightings of Neandertaloids, which are usually known locally as Wildmen or Bushmen, suggest that their distribution is limited to a small band of forests in central Asia and wilderness areas in North America's Pacific Northwest, as well as occasional appearances elsewhere in wild North America.

Neandertaloids average about 6 feet tall and have a stocky,

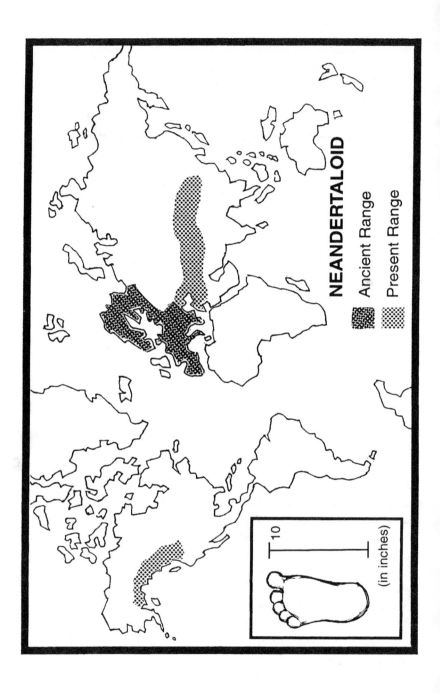

NEANDERTALOID

Ancient Range

Present Range

10

(in inches)

muscular build. Their bodies sport a reddish hair, and males generally have abundant facial hair, often with a fringe beard. The beards of this class are a clear diagnostic trait. All Neandertaloids have heavy browridges and a large, broad nose. Their feet vary from 7 to 15 inches long and are 4 to 8 inches wide. They have five toes, all about the same size and evenly spread, though their big toes angle slightly outward like those in fossil Neandertal footprints—but not at all like an ape's.

Neandertaloids are shy but curious, avoiding most contact with humans. This retiring behavior may be interpreted as a sign of intelligence. They are sometimes seen wearing skins and often make elaborate use of primitive-looking weapons such as axes, bows and arrows. Their habits are diurnal or crepuscular, their homes limited to shelters and caves, and their calls suggestive of a primitive form of communication.

Anthropologists tell us that the Neandertals, whose fossils were first discovered in Germany about one hundred fifty years ago, were a very successful species (or subspecies—there is a great debate about this). Within the last couple of years, new fossil finds have confirmed that Neandertals were contemporaries with modern humans and in some locations, survived alongside moderns until about 30,000 years ago. But ancient legends and folklore suggest that Neandertal interactions with modern man may have occurred much more recently. *The Epic of Gilgamesh,* for example, is a classic story from southern Babylonia, produced about four thousand years ago, and is the earliest hairy hominid story to appear in human literature. Gilgamesh's captured "friend," whom he named "Enkidu," was probably a Neandertal. The hairy, wild-with-the-gazelles Enkidu was first seduced by a modern Babylonian woman, then "trained" to associate with King Gilgamesh, and finally learned to do the king's bidding in battle. This is exactly what we might expect in an encounter between a Neandertal and a *Homo sapiens.*

Though the first modern artists' reconstructions of Neandertal were based on a man with a form of bone disease, there is no mistaking the striking pose these heavily built men and women took. With thicker bones, larger browridges, and larger brains by volume than *Homo sapiens,* Neandertals are somewhat "subhuman" in looks but perhaps not so in intelligence. In any case, with bodies so much hairier than those of modern humans, the Neandertal seems to be an ideal candidate for some of the more familiar Wildman sightings reported today.

5.
ERECTUS HOMINID

 The Erectus Hominid is probably the least known of the world's mystery hominids. The reason for this is simple: most of the beings in this class have in the past been misidentified as Neandertal. In Asia, for example, Russian, Chinese, Vietnamese and French researchers have all used the Neandertal to answer most of their unknown hominid questions, when, in fact, the Erectus Hominids appear to be responsible for the majority of the sightings reported.

The Erectus Hominids reside in lowlands within a wide range of habitats but are otherwise restricted to Pakistan, China, Southeast Asia, and perhaps Australia. They are known regionally by such names as Wild Men, Wild People, Lost Tribe, Stinky Ones, *almas, barmanu,* and *yeren.*

The Erectus Hominids are human-sized to about 6 feet tall. Their bodies are also within the standard human range with a slight barreling of the chest. They are partially to fully hairy, with head hair longer than their body hair. The males of the class normally display a semierect penis.

The head and face of the Erectus Hominid has a slightly Mongoloid appearance. An extremely important diagnostic feature of this class is its upturned nose. The feet have five toes, but the tracks of this retiring species are rarely mentioned, recorded, or publicized, as they tend to be on the small side of the human

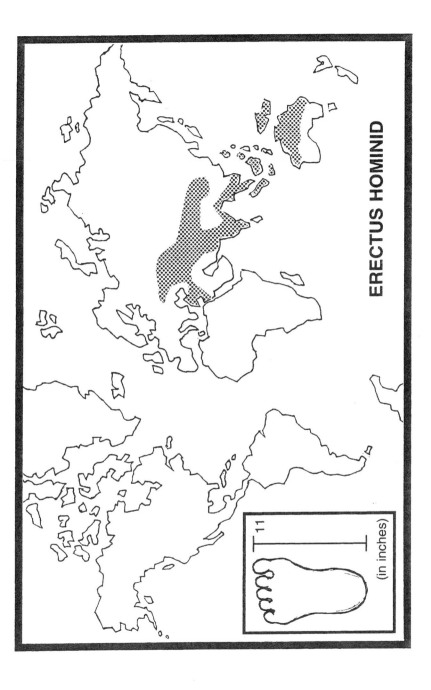

ERECTUS HOMINID

11

(in inches)

range, although somewhat wider. Confusion occurs because large Neandertal tracks are sometimes found in the same regions as sightings of the Erectus Hominid, but these tracks are not directly associated with the specific sightings of the Erectus Hominid.

The Erectus Hominid exhibits a unique sleeping position that is characteristic of these beings. They sleep with their knees and elbows drawn up under them and their hands wrapped around the back of their neck. They lie down on all fours, in other words, using the knees, hands, and elbows to rest slightly off the ground. Ivan T. Sanderson and Mark A. Hall have noted that this special sleeping position produces a prominent pad on the heel of the hand, as well as on the knees and elbows. These "pads" are found in the Central Asian varieties of the Erectus Hominid but apparently not in the subtropical ones.

The Erectus Hominid is probably among the least intelligent of the truly hominid (versus hominoid) beings in this field guide. They are retiring creatures with an omnivorous diet, who infrequently wear clothes and often exude a fierce body odor. They occasionally use very primitive tools such as sticks, clubs, and hand stones.

The *Homo erectus* of Java apeman and Peking man fame is the original small-brained, sloping but bipedal, and incorrectly labeled "missing link" so often discussed in early popular articles about prehistoric people. They have been found in fossil form in Asia, Europe, and Africa. The realization that *Homo erectus* might still be alive has been around for more than a half century within the field of cryptozoology, but other researchers have not been quick to endorse such notions. Back in 1945, W. C. Osman Hill thought some of the accounts coming out of Sumatra and Sri Lanka could be relict diminutive representatives of *Homo erectus*. But then the era of the Neandertals took over in popular culture, just as reports flourished of man-sized hominoids in Asia, and little more was said of *Homo erectus* on that continent—until the 1990s when Mark A. Hall began again to focus on the Erectus Hominid in Asia.

6.
PROTO-PYGMY

The term Proto-Pygmy describes the smallest of the world's unknown hominids. These very unique "Little People," as they are sometimes called, seem both humanlike, only small, yet nonhuman at the same time, mostly due to their hairiness and swiftness. Proto-Pygmies inhabit tropical forests, seashores, and swamps and range from southern Asia to Oceania, Africa, North America, and Latin America. They are locally known by such names as *alux, agogwe, teh-lma, séhité, sedapa,* and *shiru.*

Proto-Pygmies are smaller than most humans, varying from tiny to never more than 5.5 feet in height. They are usually slender with thick black or red fur, which is quite different from their often long, manelike head hair. There is a strange "ancient" look to their face, which is humanlike but not human, according to witnesses. They have small feet, no longer than five inches, and very small or pointed heels. Their five toes are subequal, meaning they are not in alignment across the end of the foot.

Proto-Pygmies are nervous creatures, both wary and inquisitive in their human interactions. They run fast and are very capable swimmers and tree-climbers. Usually they are seen at night, often traveling in family groups or pairs. Their diet includes insects, fish, fruits, leaves, berries, and small animals, especially frogs and snails. They are rarely seen with clothing and infrequently bear primitive tools and weapons. Their vocalizations suggest a primitive form of language.

What are the Proto-Pygmies? Theories are wide-ranging. Some North American Bigfoot researchers suggest they are simply "baby Bigfoot," even though their tracks are small with pointed heels and display a very uneven toe line—features that are diagnostically distinctive of the Proto-Pygmy. British prima-

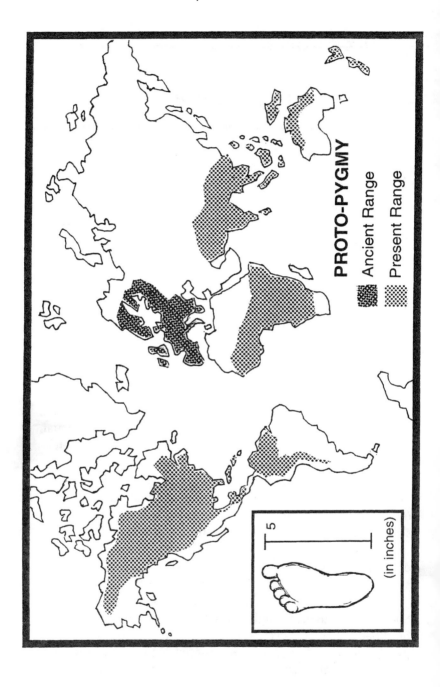

PROTO-PYGMY

Ancient Range

Present Range

(in inches)

5

tologist W. C. Osman Hill, as also noted in the Erectus Hominid class description, felt the Proto-Pygmies of Sri Lanka were a small form of *Homo erectus*. Bernard Heuvelmans, who was trained as a zoologist, thinks that some of the little people reports out of Africa could be relict populations of australopithecines. But others, like Ivan T. Sanderson, believe that some Proto-Pygmies might simply be unclassified pygmy *Homo sapiens* that have retreated into the rain forests and tropical mountain valleys of Africa or Asia. In general, the elusive nature of the Proto-Pygmies has given us little firm evidence of their fossil affinities and species relationships.

7.
UNKNOWN PONGID

Pongid is a generic term meaning nonhuman ape, and includes bonobos, chimpanzees, gorillas, and orangutans. So those mystery primates which display a pongid nature, including the classic Abominable Snowmen reports, are described in this field guide as Unknown Pongids. Tales of these apelike creatures are found among native peoples from the Louisiana Choctaw Indians, where they are known as *kashehotapalo,* to the Kenyan Wa-Sanje tribe, where they are called *ngoloko.* Other popular names for these creatures around the world include Nape, Coleman's Ape, Skunk Ape, Yeti, *kikomba,* and *apamandi.* Asian folktales of the Yeti and *met-teh* go back thousands of years.

Unknown Pongids are typically 5 to 6 feet tall, but can be up to 8 feet in height. They have larger-than-human-sized robust bodies with short legs and long arms. These pongids are characterized by a small conical head and bullneck. Some accounts describe a naked black face with fanged canines and a squashed-in nose, all shadowed by heavy browridges. Some balding is re-

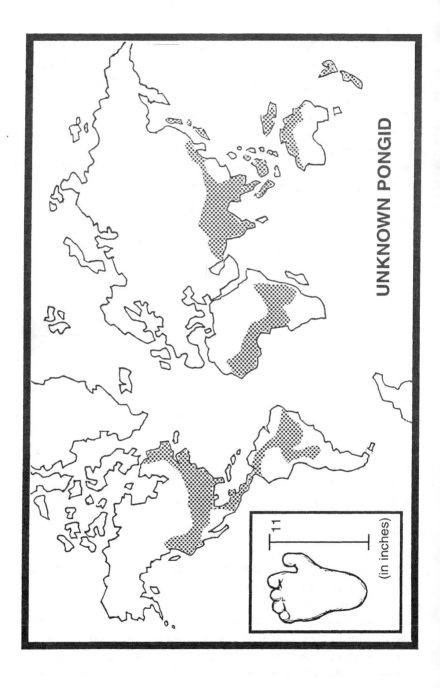

UNKNOWN PONGID

11

(in inches)

ported, as often happens in chimpanzees. Otherwise they have fairly long, coarse, shaggy hair overall. Its color varies from black to dark brown to red with very infrequent near-albinos. Some Unknown Pongids seem to have a light-colored band of hair or a different hair pattern around their midsection.

Unknown Pongids are distinguished by their very nonhuman, extremely apelike feet, which range from 6.5 to 11.5 inches wide by 9.5 to 17.5 inches long (the average footprint is 9 by 11 inches). Some forms display a squarish heel. They all have five-toed feet, with a large second toe and the big toe out at an angle. Knuckle prints have also been found.

These mystery pongids are nocturnal creatures, though they can sometimes be seen at dusk. They walk bipedally or drop to all fours, traveling widely. They are also strong swimmers, which is atypical for known apes. Their diet shows a preference for insects, snails, and small animals, though these lone hunters may also kill larger game. They sometimes emit a very strong odor, hence the name skunk ape, which they have acquired in some parts of the world.

The Unknown Pongid habitat is typically an upper mountain forest, though not above the tree line. They also can be found in woodlands, forested valleys, and bottomland swamps. Unknown Pongids appear to live in built nests or deserted structures. They seem somewhat inquisitive in their encounters with humans and can be temperamental, displaying real or simulated attacks if aroused or frightened. Their calls include trumpeting, hooting, and loud wailing; they sometimes yelp in the late afternoon or early evening.

Many researchers now link these Unknown Pongids to prehistoric dryopithecines, although it has not always been so. In the 1950s, not finding any suitable fossil affinities, Bernard Heuvelmans assigned the "youth-sized ape" form of the Yeti the new name *Dinanthropoides nivalis*. But current thought has shifted to incorporate all of the unknown pongids under the umbrella of the dryopithecines, a very successful group of early apes. In the 1960s, Loren Coleman first theorized that the so-called chimpanzee-like version of the skunk apes and other unknown pongids (which are not Bigfoot) from the southern and midwestern United States were examples of modern representatives of the genus *Dryopithecus.* Concurrently, Mark A. Hall began writing about unknown giant apes in Africa, linking them to *Dryopithecus (Proconsul) nyanzae,* and later, in discussions about the unknown pongid Yeti, noted a relationship to the fossil finds of *Dryopithecus indicus.*

8.
GIANT MONKEY

Some of the mystery primate reports from around the world clearly describe what appear to be enormous monkeys. We will use the quite appropriate, long-established term "Giant Monkey" to describe this group of reports. Although Giant Monkey reports are widespread, the best evidence of their existence comes from the temperate regions (rather than the jungles or rain forests) of Asia and the Americas.

Ancient folkloric traditions frame the recent encounters of Giant Monkeys in Asia, where they are known by such names as *kra-dhan* and *bekk-bok.* The Abbé Pierre Bordet has pointed out that the mountain range that includes Mt. Everest is called by the Indians *Mahalanguar Himal,* meaning "Mountains of the Great Monkeys," not due to the reports of the classic Abominable Snowmen from the area but because of the concurrent traditions of Giant Monkeys.

Accounts from South America of unknown giant monkeys, known variously as *salvaje* or *isnashi,* among other names, also date back to the nineteenth century—prior, it should be noted, to the confusion caused by an apparent hoax, the famous photograph of a 5-foot-tall upright "ape" supposedly taken in Venezuela by the French explorer François de Loys in 1920. In North

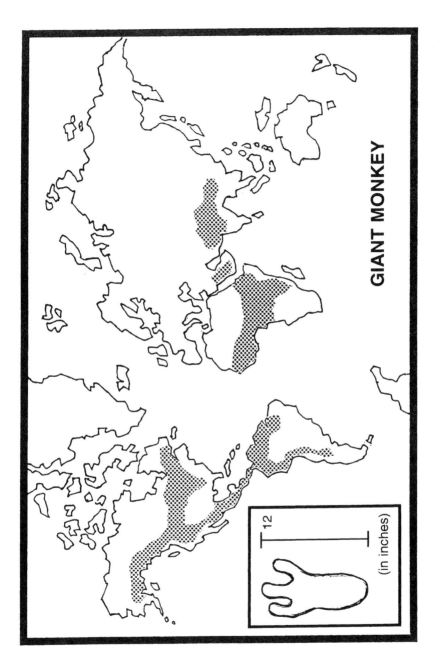

GIANT MONKEY

12

(in inches)

America the sightings of these Giant Monkeys are sometimes referred to as "Devil Monkeys," while others sometimes appear to observers to be "kangaroos."

Giant Monkeys are generally 4 to 6 feet tall; the smaller ones (juveniles) often resemble wallabies or "baby kangaroos." They have muscular bodies with barrel chests, arms thicker than a man's, very strong legs, and a thick tail. Their faces are often described as being doglike or baboonlike, with dark piercing eyes and pointed ears. They have short to shaggy hair, varying in color from black to red, often with a heavy coat around the shoulders in males.

Giant Monkeys have large flat feet that tend to narrow somewhat as they lengthen in adulthood. Their footprints are usually about 12 inches long, but tracks up to 15 inches have been found. Their foot bears three rounded toes, usually of the same size and length, with regular spacing between each one.

Giant Monkeys can be aggressive toward humans and dogs; eyewitnesses view them as being mean or forceful in their appearances. However, they have learned to be cautious most of the time, for survival reasons, and thus are not often encountered. They are diurnal primates living in pulled-together nests or old human buildings. They use saltation, or leaping, to move around. They are generally thought to be vegetarians but sometimes bother livestock and small game. Giant Monkeys exhibit a wide range of simian hoots, calls, screeches, whistles, and "blood-chilling screams." Sometimes a minor odor is reported in their presence.

In terms of fossil affinities, Bernard Heuvelmans pointed out that there have been finds in India of a giant baboon *Simopithecus,* twice as big as the largest baboon, literally a giant form of *Theropithecus gelada,* the gelada baboons of Ethiopia. He noted that the paleoanthropological discoveries of Robert Broom included a similar giant baboon *Dinopithecus,* and Heuvelmans asked in the 1950s if these two could have something to do with the native legends of the Nandi bear. Beginning in the 1970s, Mark A. Hall stated that the American version of the Giant Monkey seemed identical to *Simopithecus.* Recent fossil finds of a giant howler–spider monkey in South America have focused some attention on that extinct form, but it has not yet been determined whether it was as bulky as the Giant Monkey reported in modern Neotropical accounts.

9.
MERBEING

The Merbeing, or water creature, is perhaps the most traditional of all the undiscovered nonhuman primates. Perhaps surprisingly the Mermaids and Mermen of ancient lore are still being seen today, though, apparently, in far fewer numbers. Yet this group of water-connected beings ranges far beyond the Merpeople of yore and includes such varieties as the Sea Ape of the Bering Sea, the scaly-looking but actually hairy and misnamed Lizard Men, and the fiery-eyed Latino phenomenon known as the *chupacabras*. While a growing Hispanic population in the Americas is only now actively examining and discussing their Merbeing sightings, Asians have been aware of their *kappas* and other Merbeings for centuries.

Merbeings appear to come in two varieties. The marine subclass is distinguished by a finlike appendage, while the other, mostly freshwater, subclass is characterized by an angular foot with a high instep and three pointed toes. The freshwater creatures are often found venturing onto land and are far more aggressive and dangerous, being carnivorous, than their calmer marine cousins.

Merbeings vary in height from dwarf to man-sized. Their bodies are strong, but not stocky or bulky. The marine variety has very smooth skin, sometimes with a very short "fur," while the freshwater variety occasionally has patchy hair growths that appear "like leaves" or "scaly." In both subclasses, the hair is often

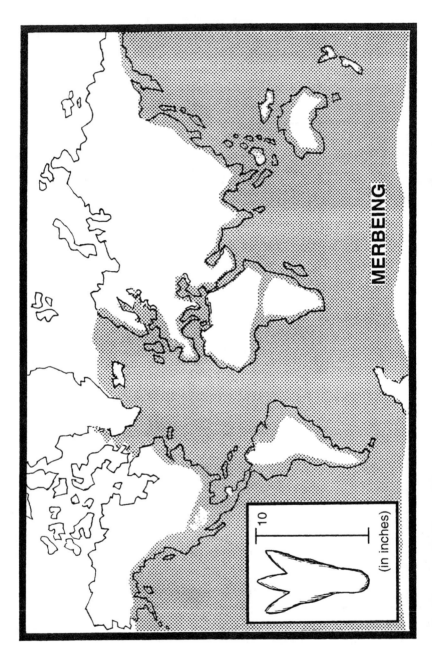

MERBEING

10

(in inches)

maned, though some exhibit almost complete hair cover, especially in the *chupacabras* kin. Merbeings in general have eyes that are usually oval or almond-shaped, perhaps due to their watery origins. These mostly nocturnal creatures have a singsong vocalization, which has been reported almost universally from Eurasia to Africa.

Freshwater Merbeings often display a row of spikes down along the back, a rather uncommon but not unknown feature among primates. In the potto, a cat-sized loris from south-central Africa, the spines of the last neck vertebra and first vertebra of the thorax penetrate the skin and are capped with horny spines. When threatened, the spikes stand up so a predator can't bite the potto on the neck. So it appears to be with some Merbeings. In fact, the resemblance between freshwater Merbeings and the potto nearly extends down to the toes of their feet. While Merbeings appear to be three-toed, the potto has an enormous big toe that points in the opposite direction to its third, fourth and fifth toes, and its second toe is nothing more than a lump bearing a cleaning claw. So much for primates not having weird digits and spines on their backs.

The whole body of lore on Merbeings appears to have some basis in reality and is not all myth. Credible sightings have occurred. On the other hand, the increased activity or visibility of the *chupacabras* and the decreased accounts of ocean-dwelling Mermaids and Mermen may signal a shift toward the successful survival of the more aggressive freshwater, land-oriented subclass. Sightings of the scary, triple-toed Honey Island swamp monster in Louisiana, the three-fingered and three-toed Thetis Lake monster in Canada, and similarly digited Scape Ore Swamp Lizard Man in South Carolina, plus the *chupacabras,* suggests that the most dangerous Merbeing variety is presently at the head of its class.

NORTH
AMERICA

REGION: *North America*
CLASS: *Neo-Giant*
TYPE: *Bigfoot, Sasquatch, oh-mah*
DISTINGUISHING CHARACTERISTIC: *pointed head*

DESCRIPTIVE INCIDENT:
DATE: *October 20, 1967*
LOCATION: *Bluff Creek, California*
WITNESSES: *Roger Patterson, Robert Gimlin*

While riding in the Six Rivers National Forest early one afternoon, Roger Patterson, an expert rodeo rider, and Robert Gimlin, a part–Native American outdoorsman, rounded a bend and spotted a large upright creature on one of the creek's sandbars. The dark, full-figured creature was covered with short hair (even on its large pendulous breasts) and possessed a sagittal crest. This bony ridge on top of the head, which supports heavy jaw muscles, has only been found, in primates, on certain fossil hominoids (especially *Paranthropus*) and among a few male modern apes, baboons, and other large current species.

Patterson's small Welsh pony smelled the creature and reared, bringing both pony and rider to the ground. But Patterson got up, grabbed his camera from the saddlebag, and while running toward the creature, took 24 feet of color film with the rented 16mm handheld Kodak movie camera. The creature walked steadily away into the forest, turning its head once toward the camera. Gimlin, meanwhile, remained on his horse, a 30.06 rifle in hand, fearing his friend might be attacked. But the Bigfoot soon disappeared into the woods. The men then tracked it for three miles, but lost it in the heavy undergrowth. Immediately after the filming and in the days that followed, casts of the tracks were taken from the many footprints—each 14.5 inches long by 6 inches wide—the creature had left in the sandy blue-gray clay soil.

Similar footprints found in this area over the years had drawn the two men from Yakima, Washington, to search the area and now they had 952 frames of color film to support the existence of this 6- to 7-foot-tall, 500- to 700-pound creature. While scientists who have examined this footage remain divided on its authenticity to date—claims about men-in-suits from Hollywood notwithstanding—no firm evidence has surfaced to cast serious doubts on the film or the events that produced it. In particular, the apparent movement of the creature's muscles beneath its hair argues strongly against a hoax.

Native Americans, First Nation Canadians, and Alaskan Inuits all have legends going back centuries of giant hairy men and women like the one seen in this film (see book cover).

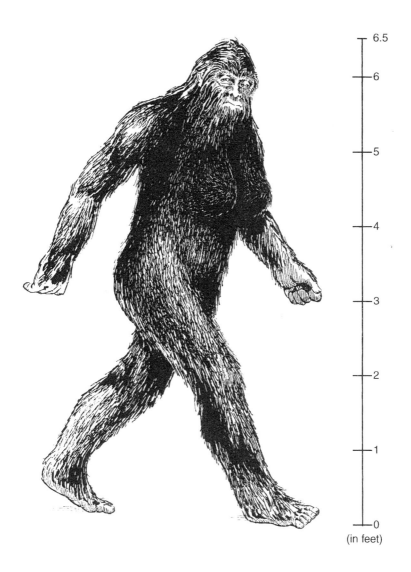

6.5

6

5

4

3

2

1

0
(in feet)

43

REGION: *North America*	**DESCRIPTIVE INCIDENT:**
CLASS: *True Giant*	**DATE:** *June 1965*
TYPE: *Pitt Lake Giant*	**LOCATION:** *Pitt Lake, British Columbia, Canada*
DISTINGUISHING CHARACTERISTIC: *four-toed tracks*	**WITNESSES:** *Ron Welch and his brother*

D uring the last week of the month, in a valley northwest of Pitt Lake, two prospectors chanced upon a set of huge tracks in the snow. The four-toed tracks were obviously fresh as their edges were still sharp in the bright noonday sun. Each footprint measured an enormous 24 inches long and 12 inches across. The bottom of each impression was flat and had a pink tint.

The stride made by the creature's well-separated left and right footprints was about twice that of a man's. Outside the footprints were some puzzling heavy groves as deep as the footprints themselves, and in the middle of the prints was another mark suggesting that the creature had been dragging something wide but not very heavy.

The brothers followed these prints up to a small ice-covered lake whose surface was broken by a single large hole. As the two men started walking around the lake they spotted a creature watching them from the other side "just a stone's throw away." The creature did not move and neither did the prospectors, who sat down and had a cigarette and chocolate bar, while one drew a sketch of the giant.

Using trees nearby as a scale, the men estimated the creature's size. One guessed was that it was between 10 and 12 feet tall; the other thought it was 12 to 14 feet high. By either measure, the creature was enormous, its head resting atop square-set shoulders on a very wide frame. It was covered with auburn-colored hair, which seemed thinner on its arms and longer on its head. But its hands, which were the shape and size of canoe paddles and hung on arms that reached below the creature's knees, appeared distinctly yellow.

Because the creature remained immobile, the prospectors decided to move on. When they returned later in the day, the creature was gone, though more tracks covered the area.

Stories of tall creatures with enormous footprints date back to 1829 and Creek Indian traditions in the Okefenokee Swamp of Georgia. Reports of these giants come from across the country, including South Carolina in 1977 and Pennsylvania in 1993. But most sightings of True Giants in North America come from the high mountains of the west and the spruce forests of the north.

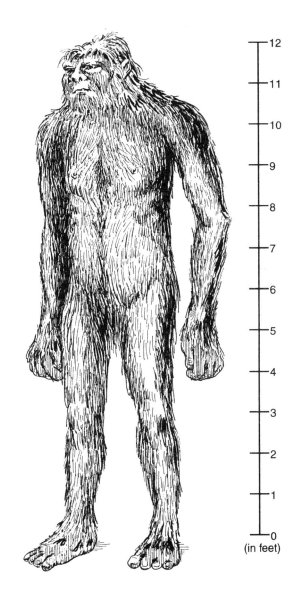

```
— 12
— 11
— 10
— 9
— 8
— 7
— 6
— 5
— 4
— 3
— 2
— 1
— 0
(in feet)
```

45

REGION: *North America*	**DESCRIPTIVE INCIDENT:**
CLASS: *Marked Hominid*	**DATE:** *Late August 1972–*
TYPE: *Pennsylvania Creature*	*mid-January 1973*
DISTINGUISHING CHARACTERISTIC:	**LOCATION:** *Westmoreland County,*
pot-bellied	*Pennsylvania*
	WITNESS: *Professor "Jan Klement"*

A small-town earth sciences professor had a series of encounters with a large hairy creature, beginning with some simple sightings near his cabin in the woods of southwestern Pennsylvania and eventually leading to closer contacts with it starting late in September 1972. The professor was able to lure the creature close to his shanty by putting out apples. For almost four months, the creature tolerated the professor's very proximate observations.

The visiting beast was neither apelike nor manlike. It stood 7 feet tall and was covered in short brown hair with slightly longer hair on the head, under the arms, and in the pubic area. Its large eyes and expressive mouth sat in a face that was not primitive or animal-like, but the short hair that grew from the eyes down gave the appearance of a mask. The arms did not reach below the knees. It had a powerful body with well-developed leg and shoulder muscles, flat buttocks, 13-inch humanlike feet, and a 6-inch-long penis. The most notable feature was its protruding stomach. The creature smelled like a damp dog.

The professor observed the creature eating and excreting, as well as killing a deer and small animals. It grew to trust the professor's presence but was always cautious, never left tracks, and invariably made itself scarce when metal objects, cameras, or other people were near. But finally, in mid-January 1973, the professor found the creature dead and buried it. He has since returned to the burial spot but cannot find any trace of it. It appears to have been dug up. Researcher Mark A. Hall considers the "Jan Klement" case one of the best recent examples of a *Homo gardarensis* encounter in eastern North America.

Beginning in the summer of 1973, Westmoreland County, Pennsylvania, experienced a high number of encounters with 7- to 8-foot-tall hairy upright creatures. Between July 1973 and February 1974, at least fifty individual eyewitnesses reported sightings of Bigfoot-like creatures in twenty-two different incidents. These sightings involved mostly single creatures; one involved two, and another involved three in an apparent family group. Most were dark colored, but one was white, another one was tan, and another had a white mane. In three of the encounters, the creatures were shot at; blood was found in one case.

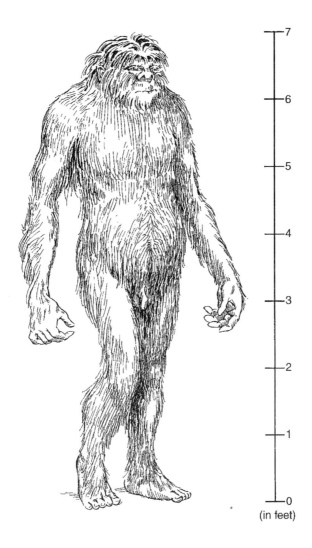

```
— 7

— 6

— 5

— 4

— 3

— 2

— 1

— 0
(in feet)
```

47

REGION: *North America*	**DESCRIPTIVE INCIDENT:**
CLASS: *Marked Hominid*	**DATE:** *August 1970*
TYPE: *Old Yellow Top, Yellow Top,*	**LOCATION:** *Cobalt, Ontario, Canada*
PreCambrian Shield Man	**WITNESSES:** *Aimee Latreille, Larry*
DISTINGUISHING CHARACTERISTIC:	*Cormack, and others*
light-colored mane	

The most recent sighting of "Old Yellow Top" occurred in early August 1970, when the creature almost caused the deaths of twenty-seven miners on their way to work the graveyard shift at Cobalt Lode. Bus driver Aimee Latreille said he was startled by a dark form that walked across the road in front of him, making him lose control of the bus, nearly plunging it down a nearby rock cut.

"At first I thought it was a big bear," Latreille said. "But then it turned to face the headlights and I could see some light hair, almost down to the shoulders. It couldn't have been a bear. I have heard of this thing before but never believed it. Now I am sure." One of the miners at the front of the bus also caught a brief glimpse of the creature. It also looked like a bear to Larry Cormack, "but it didn't walk like one. It was kind of half stooped over." As often happens with such stories, some news reporters joked about the case being a hoax.

The earliest report of the creature, initially nicknamed PreCambrian Shield Man, came from a group of men building the headframe at the Violet Mine, east of Cobalt, in September 1906. Seventeen years later, in late July of 1923, two prospectors, J. A. MacAuley and Lorne Wilson, were taking test samples from their mining claims northeast of the Wettlaufer Mine near Cobalt when they saw what looked like a bear picking at a blueberry patch. When Wilson threw a stone at the creature, it stood up, growled, then ran away. "Its head was kind of yellow and the rest of it was black like a bear, all covered with hair," noted Wilson.

The creature's third appearance occurred in April 1946, when a woman and her son, living near Gillies Depot, saw the half-man, half-beast as they were walking the railroad tracks into Cobalt. The woman said that she spotted a dark, hairy animal with a "light" head ambling off the tracks into the bush near Gillies Lake. She said it walked almost like a man.

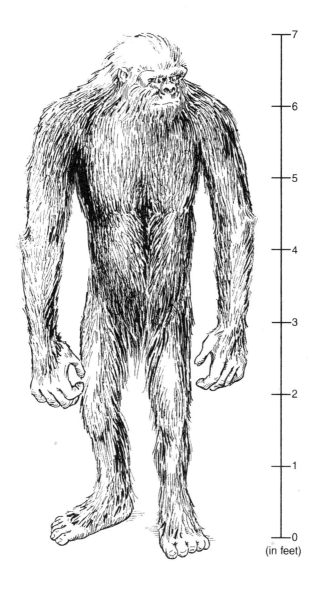

REGION: *North America*
CLASS: *Marked Hominid*
TYPE: *Momo, Sister Lakes Monster, Monroe Monster*
DISTINGUISHING CHARACTERISTIC: *hair covering eyes*

DESCRIPTIVE INCIDENT:
DATE: *July 11, 1972*
LOCATION: *Louisiana, Missouri*
WITNESSES: *Terry, Wally, and Doris Harrison*

The Momo scare began at about 3:30 P.M. on a sunny day near the outskirts of a little town of 4,600 inhabitants. ("Momo" is short for "Missouri Monster.") Terry and his brother, Wally, were playing in their yard when their older sister, Doris, who was inside, heard a scream. She looked out the bathroom window and saw by a tree a creature flecked with blood with a dead dog under its arm. Doris and Terry described it as being 6 or 7 feet tall, black, and hairy. They could not see its face, as its head and face were covered with hair. Nor could they see a neck. The creature "stood like a man but it didn't look like one," Doris said, and soon waddled off with the dog still under its arm. The Harrisons' own dog grew violently ill afterward, vomiting for three hours, and neighbors spoke of dogs that had disappeared.

Three days later, the children's father, Ellis Harrison, smelled terrible odors and heard horrible howls around the area. Then on July 21, Ellis Minor, who lived on nearby River Road, heard his dogs bark and, thinking it was another dog, flashed a light out into his yard. When he stepped outside, he saw a 6-foot-tall, erect, black-haired creature. The beast then quickly dashed into the woods. Two weeks later, the sightings ceased.

In July 1971, a year before the Momo scare, Joan Mills and Mary Ryan saw a hairy half-ape, half-man on River Road near Louisiana, Missouri, but reports of hairy half-human creatures had actually circulated in the area as far back as the 1940s. A comparable creature with the same physique and hair in its face has also been seen in 1964 in Michigan, where it is known as the Sister Lakes Monster. In another incident, which took place on August 13, 1965, a huge, dark creature with hair all over its body and face attacked Christine Van Acker, who was sitting with her mother in their car near Monroe, Michigan.

These creatures are often referred to as "Eastern Bigfoot." Nevertheless, in temperament, interactions with dogs, body build, and the clear lack of similar facial features, these nonmontane hominids appear to be very different from the classic Bigfoot of the Pacific Northwest.

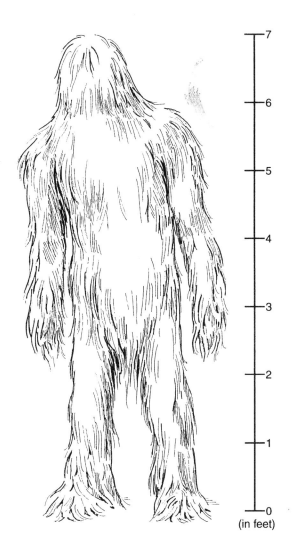

7

6

5

4

3

2

1

0
(in feet)

51

REGION: *North America*	**DESCRIPTIVE INCIDENT**
CLASS: *Neandertaloid*	DATE: *April–June 1964*
TYPE: *Nuk-luk ("Man of the Bush"),*	LOCATION: *Nahanni Butte, Northwest*
nakani ("Bad Indian"), bushman	*Territories, Canada*
DISTINGUISHING CHARACTERISTIC:	WITNESSES: *John Baptist, several men,*
long, dark beard	*and a boy named Jerry*

One day John Baptist, an Indian from the Ft. Laird settlement, and several fellow Native Canadians who were trapping in the area of the butte at the junction of the Liard and South Nahanni Rivers, came upon a man-shaped creature that was rather strong-looking and sported a long, dark beard. It wore no clothes, and appeared rather shy. As the trappers approached, it uttered a low growl and fled.

Two months later, near the edge of Ft. Simpson, there was a report of a similar creature. One evening, at about 9 P.M., a dog belonging to Jerry (age fourteen) began barking. When the boy and his father went out with a flashlight to find out what was wrong, they were surprised to see a rather small, dark, upright, hominid creature covered with black hair on its head, upper body, and legs. It had a black head, slightly pointed at the back, and a light brown face with a small black nose. Though it, too, had a very long, brown beard that went down to its waist, this creature wore some kind of ankle-high boots and a piece of moose skin around its waist, and it carried a stone club.

The creature stood for a moment in the flashlight's glare but departed rapidly when the dog began to bark again. The *nuk-luk* crossed the boy's property, then crossed the road in front of the house. Several bystanders also spotted it and gave chase, but when the creature saw them, it immediately dashed into the bush.

Frank Graves of the American Expeditionary Society collected these sightings and investigated the long traditions of *nuk-luk, nakani,* and Bushmen that are said to inhabit the Nahanni Valley. This valley has also been nicknamed the "Headless Valley" because it has been the site of strange disappearances and beheadings of prospectors for the last two hundred years, with a dozen documented vanishings recorded since 1904. Four of those bodies turned up without heads. The folklore surrounding the Nahanni Valley and the legends of the Bushmen with their whistling calls and bootlike footprints have been entwined for some time. Reports of the Bushmen, an alleged ancient tribe with a nasty reputation, range from this part of the Northwest Territories through the Yukon to the Kenai Peninsula of Alaska.

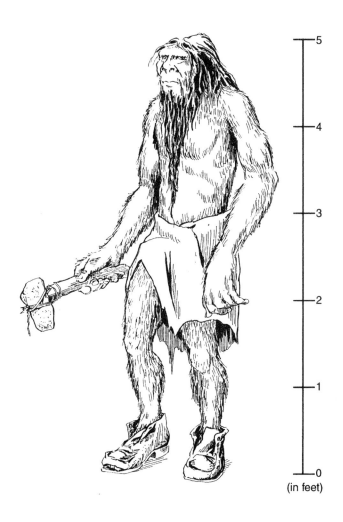

5

4

3

2

1

0
(in feet)

53

REGION: *North America*
CLASS: *Erectus Hominid*
TYPE: *Minnesota Iceman, Bozo,*
Homo pongoides
DISTINGUISHING CHARACTERISTIC:
upturned nose

DESCRIPTIVE INCIDENT:
DATE: *December 17, 1968*
LOCATION: *Rollingstone, Minnesota*
WITNESSES: *Terry Cullen, Ivan T.*
Sanderson, Bernard Heuvelmans,
among others

During the autumn of 1967, college zoology major Terry Cullen spotted an extraordinary exhibit in Milwaukee—an apparently authentic fresh corpse of a hairy manlike animal. After trying unsuccessfully to interest mainstream scientists, he alerted Ivan T. Sanderson, whose guest in New Jersey at the time was the Belgian cryptozoologist Bernard Heuvelmans. The two immediately traveled to see firsthand what exhibitor Frank Hansen was showing at fairs and shopping centers across the American Midwest. For twenty-five cents people could see the "man left over from the Ice Age" that Hansen kept frozen in a block of ice in a refrigerated glass coffin.

For three days, Sanderson and Heuvelmans examined the creature in Hansen's cramped trailer. The specimen was an adult male, 6 feet tall, with large hands and feet. Its skin was a corpselike white and covered with very dark brown hair 3 to 4 inches long. The creature had apparently been shot through one eye, which dangled on its face, but it also had a gaping wound and open fracture on its left arm. Smelling putrefaction where some of the flesh had been exposed because of melting ice, the two concluded the creature was authentic.

Hansen wanted the discovery kept quiet, but both Heuvelmans and Sanderson wrote scientific papers on the creature within the year. Heuvelmans named it *Homo pongoides.*

Then the original body disappeared, and a model, apparently made in California, replaced it, with various Hollywood makeup artists claiming to have created the Iceman. But Sanderson and Heuvelmans knew of at least fifteen technical differences between the original and the replacement, thanks to photographs of the traveling exhibit taken by Mark A. Hall and Loren Coleman. When the Smithsonian Institution and the FBI got involved, Hansen explained that the creature was owned by a millionaire and declined to have it examined further.

The Iceman appears to be an "accidental," in other words, not of local origin. Heuvelmans theorized it was a Neandertal killed in Vietnam during the war and smuggled into the United States in a "body bag." Its Erectus-like features, however, match quite well some of the reports coming out of Central Asia.

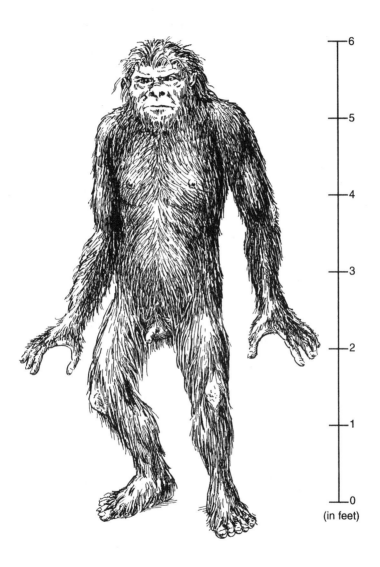

6

5

4

3

2

1

0
(in feet)

55

REGION: *North America*
CLASS: *Unknown Pongid*
TYPE: *Nape, Skunk Ape, booger*
DISTINGUISHING CHARACTERISTIC:
swinging arms

DESCRIPTIVE INCIDENT:
DATE: *February 1970*
LOCATION: *near Central, Arkansas*
WITNESS: *Nathan Russell*

N athan Russell was going to a neighbor's home when he came across an animal sitting in a tree. Suddenly, it jumped down, letting its arms swing in front of it like an ape, and making a heavy breathing noise. Scared, Russell just stood staring at the beast for about three minutes while it stared back. Then he started to run and the thing chased after him, getting to within 6 feet before Russell came to his friend's home, and the apelike beast departed.

The creature was about 5 feet 8 inches tall and had arms as long as Russell's own. Its head seemed bald and it had no hair on its neck. "From the neck down, there was long hair, and then halfway down, the hair was short like a hound's," said Russell. It had humanlike ears and "eyes like a hog's."

Similar apelike animals have been reported in other southern and midwestern states for years. The various names given to these creatures often mask the apes' essential similarities. For example, Howard Dresson gave bananas to a "chimpanzee" that visited him regularly near his Oklahoma home from 1967 through 1970. And during 1979, North Carolina had several encounters with "Knobby." Arkansas's "Fouke Monster" made famous by the *Legend of Boggy Creek* films, appears to have been one or more of the same apelike animals, also called *boogers* locally, seen by Nathan Russell in Arkansas.

These North American Apes—dubbed "Napes" by Loren Coleman in the 1960s—appear to be a population of chimpanzee-like apes that inhabit the bottomlands and vast network of closed-canopy deciduous and mixed forests of the Mississippi Valley and its tributaries. Some encounters are dimly remembered in regional folklore and in twentieth-century reports of "gorillas" and "chimps." In 1962, Coleman found a footprint complete with an opposed big toe (characteristic of the footprint of a lowland gorilla or a chimpanzee) in a dry creek bed near Decatur, Illinois. Similar prints have been found in Florida, Alabama, and Oklahoma.

During a series of August 1971 sightings of two chimpanzee-like apes (termed "Skunk Apes" by the media), Broward County (Florida) rabies control officer Henry Ring "found nothing but a bunch of strange tracks, like someone was walking around on his knuckles." But such knuckle-walking is exactly what one would expect of an ape.

5.5

5

4

3

2

1

0

(in feet)

REGION: *North America*
CLASS: *Unknown Pongid*
TYPE: *Lake Worth Monster, Goatman*
DISTINGUISHING CHARACTERISTIC:
all-white hair

DESCRIPTIVE INCIDENT:
DATE: *November 7, 1969*
LOCATION: *Lake Worth, Texas*
WITNESS: *Charles Buchanan*

C harles Buchanan was camped on the shores of Lake Worth when he awoke at 2 A.M. to find himself face-to-face with a strange creature. The hairy beast looked "like a cross between a human being and a gorilla or ape." Buchanan had been sleeping in the bed of his truck when the creature suddenly jerked him to the ground, sleeping bag and all. Gagging from the stench of the beast, Buchanan did the only thing he could think of: he grabbed a bag of leftover chicken and shoved it into the long-armed creature's face. The "monster" took the sack in its mouth, made some guttural sounds, and then loped off through the trees, splashed into the water, and swam off with powerful strokes toward Greer Island.

Many others had seen the Lake Worth Monster, or Goatman, in June and July of that year, according to police reports. Things had come to a head on July 10, when four units of the Fort Worth police descended on the Lake Worth area, near Greer Island, to search for a beast that had attacked six terrified residents. One, John Reichart, told of how the thing had jumped out from behind a tree and tried to grab his wife, and he had an 18-inch scratch along the side of his car to prove it. And so it was that thirty to forty residents, including law enforcement officers, showed up to look for the beast. All of a sudden, a huge apelike animal appeared at the top of an embankment near the original sightings, uttered a howl, leapt from a bluff, and threw an automobile tire and wheel some 500 feet at the group of onlookers. Everyone, including the sheriff's deputies, jumped in their cars.

Witnesses agreed it was "big, hairy, and whitish." One eyewitness, John E. Harris of Terrace Trail, said he heard a squalling, pitiful cry that didn't sound human right before the "monster" tossed the tire. Three residents claimed they fired on it and followed a trail of blood. And one local resident named Allen Plaster, owner of a clothing store, took a fuzzy photograph that showed a large, hairy white beast.

The Buchanan sighting four months later was the last documented encounter of the Lake Worth Monster. This creature appears to be a light-colored, regional variation of the Nape, the Northern American Ape.

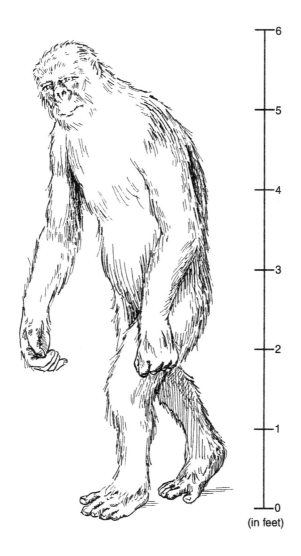

6 —

5 —

4 —

3 —

2 —

1 —

0 —
(in feet)

REGION: *North America*
CLASS: *Giant Monkey*
TYPE: *Devil Monkey, nalusa falaya*
DISTINGUISHING CHARACTERISTIC:
long, pointed ears

DESCRIPTIVE INCIDENT:
DATE: *June 26, 1997*
LOCATION: *Dunkinsville, Ohio*
WITNESS: *Debbie Cross*

D ebbie Cross lives on a wooded ridge near Peach Mountain, at the foothills of the Appalachian Mountains. To the east lies the Shawnee State Forest. Between the hours of midnight and 1 A.M. on the night in question, the witness was watching television when she heard her dogs barking outside. When she turned on the porch light, she observed a strange animal about 30 feet away near the pond in her front yard.

"It was about three to four feet tall and gray in color," she told researchers Ron Schaffner and Kenny Young. "It had large, dark eyes and rounded ears extended above the head. It had real long arms and a short tail. It made a gurgling sound. From the available light, the animal appeared to have hair or fur all over its body about one and a half inches long."

The animal looked at Cross for a few seconds then headed towards a tent on the southern part of the pond. It kind of "skipped" when it moved, Cross noted, and appeared to walk on its hind legs while using the "knuckles" of its front arms on the ground one at a time. When her two dogs then started to chase it, she called them back. The animal then headed along a barbed-wire fence and went out of view. Cross heard a screeching sound shortly afterward.

Researchers Mark A. Hall and Loren Coleman have chronicled reports of this kind for almost thirty years and refer to them as "Devil Monkeys." They appear to be a kind of giant baboon that moves by saltation, leaping as do kangaroos—and are often mistaken for them. Due to their size and means of locomotion, they have evolved a large flat foot with three rounded toes. Immature Devil Monkeys resemble marsupials such as wallabies due to convergent evolution but this similarity diminishes as they mature.

Native American folklore from Louisiana refers to swamp creatures known to the Choctaw as the *nalusa falaya,* meaning "long evil being." This being, according to Hall, is probably the Devil Monkey, as its general description mentions the characteristic long, pointed ears. Sightings of these Devil Monkeys have been reported from Alaska to New Brunswick, with a concentration of contemporary sightings in the Midwest, though this reporting pattern may not truly reflect the range distribution.

5

4

3

2

1

0

(in feet)

61

REGION: *North America*	DESCRIPTIVE INCIDENT:
CLASS: *Merbeing (freshwater)*	DATE: *August 1972*
TYPE: *Thetis Lake Monster, Lizardman, Tchimose*	LOCATION: *Thetis Lake, British Columbia, Canada*
DISTINGUISHING CHARACTERISTIC: *sharp three-toed footprints*	WITNESSES: *Gordon Pike, Robin Flewellyn, Mike Gold, Russel Van Nice*

Thetis Lake, which is near Colwood, not far from Victoria, was the scene of several "monster" reports in August 1972. The first sighting took place on August 19, when Gordon Pike and Robin Flewellyn reported seeing a 5-foot-tall bipedal beast emerge from the waters of the lake and chase them from the beach. In the process, Flewellyn was cut on the hand by one of the six razor-sharp points atop the creature's head. The Royal Canadian Mounted Police found the two boys sincere and began an investigation.

On August 23, Mike Gold and Russell Van Nice reported seeing the creature in the middle of the afternoon, across the lake from where it had appeared the previous Wednesday. The two saw the creature come out of the water momentarily, look around, then return to the water. Gold described the creature as having a "human" body, though it seemed scaly and silver-colored. He said the creature had the face of a "monster" with big ears and "a point sticking out of its head."

One of the deities of the Haidah Indians, who live on Queen Charlotte's Island, supposedly resides in the sea. *Tchimose,* as he is known, has a human face and two tails, and he wears a hat. Haidah canoeists fear this creature.

Reports of similar man-sized monsters have also emerged from many swamps in the Deep South, the Ohio River Valley, and the Delaware River Valley, going back, at least, to the last century. Distinctive, sharply pointed three-toed tracks are often found where eyewitnesses report their encounters with these bizarre upright Merbeings. The prints have been discovered in such diverse locations as Honey Island Swamp, Louisiana, and Scape Ore Swamp, North Carolina, two sites that have lengthy histories with these behaviorally aggressive and formidable beasts. Researchers are now beginning to link North American "Creatures of the Black Lagoon" cases like this one to the sightings of Latin American violent, spiky-headed *chupacabras.*

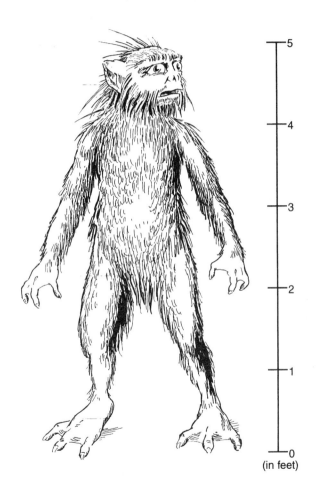

5
4
3
2
1
0
(in feet)

REGION: *North America*	**DESCRIPTIVE INCIDENT:**
CLASS: *Merbeing (marine)*	**DATE:** *August 10, 1741*
TYPE: *Sea Ape*	**LOCATION:** *Off the Shumagin Islands,*
DISTINGUISHING CHARACTERISTIC:	*Alaska*
long upper and lower lip whiskers	**WITNESS:** *Georg Wilhelm Steller*

The islands of the Aleutian chain are among the loneliest places on Earth. One of the area's earliest explorers was Georg Wilhelm Steller, a naturalist whose great voyage in the eighteenth century led to the discovery of many previously unknown plants and animals. All of the new species described in Steller's detailed diary have been corroborated—except one. "With such a record of reliability," noted the zoologist Roy Mackal, "we must attach considerable credence to [Stellar's] one and only observation" of the "Sea Ape."

On this day Steller's vessel was essentially hemmed in by wooded islands. The quiet sea was filled with numerous hair seals, sea otters, fur seals, sea lions, and porpoises—and one animal he had never seen before. Circling the boat for about two hours was an animal about 5 feet long, with a head like a dog's. It had large eyes and pointy erect ears. Whiskers hung down from its upper and lower lips. Its body was thick and round and tapered gradually toward the tail, which had two fins, the upper one twice as large as the lower, as in sharks. It had neither forefeet nor forefins. The skin of the animal was covered with thick hair, gray on its back but a reddish white on its belly.

The animal swam gracefully around the ship, stopping occasionally to raise itself one-third out of the water for a few minutes, looking, "as with admiration, first at the one and then at the other of us," noted Steller. Sometimes it came so close to the ship that they could have touched it with a pole. At one point it seized in its mouth a clump of seaweed 3 to 4 fathoms long, making "motions and monkey tricks" with it that had the crew in stitches.

Finally, Steller got a gun and fired at the animal several times "in order to get possession of it for a more accurate description." But apparently Steller missed as the animal swam away only to be seen again later, several times in different places.

What did Steller see that day? He was certainly too exacting a naturalist to have misidentified a sea otter or fur seal, especially at such close range. It could then—just possibly—have been some aquatic form of primate, as the name he bestowed upon it implies.

LATIN
AMERICA

REGION: *Latin America*	**DESCRIPTIVE INCIDENT:**
CLASS: *Neo-Giant*	**Date:** *May 1958*
TYPE: *Ucumar, ucu, ukumar-zupai,*	**LOCATION:** *Rengo, Chile*
sisemite	**WITNESSES:** *Carlos Manuel Soto and*
DISTINGUISHING CHARACTERISTIC:	*others*
giant, humanlike footprints	

Reports of South American creatures looking exactly like North America's Sasquatch and Bigfoot are rare. But similar sightings do come from the Andes. Carlos Manuel Soto and a party of campers were located at a site in Rengo, 50 miles from Santiago, Chile, when they were visited by an "ape-man." Police were called in to investigate and took affidavits. "I saw an enormous man covered with hair in the Cordilleras," states Soto's affidavit in part.

Other such creatures were seen in the region at about the same time. In 1956, a geologist found 17-inch-long, humanlike footprints at a height of over 16,000 feet on the Argentinean side of the Andes. The following year, similar foot tracks were found in the La Salta province of Argentina. These finds greatly distressed the villagers of Tolor Grande, who told newspaper reporters that they were especially disturbed by the nightly chorus of "eerie calls" coming from the Curu-Curu Mountains. The Tolor Grande residents said this was the habitat of the feared creature known as *ukumar-zupai.*

Today, stories of these hairy giants, often called *ucumar,* are still heard in Argentina. While visiting the mountainous regions of northern Argentina in 1979, the anthropologist Silva Alicia Barrios was told that the *ucumar,* or *ucu,* often screamed at cows and chickens and liked to eat *payo,* a cabbagelike plant. Some people had apparently even seen *ucumars* trap people. The "strange monkey" was said to be big, bulky, and strong. Researchers Ivan T. Sanderson and Mark A. Hall have linked the montane forest accounts of the *sisemite* near Mount Kacharul, Guatemala, to the Neo-Giants Sasquatch, Bigfoot, and *ucumar.*

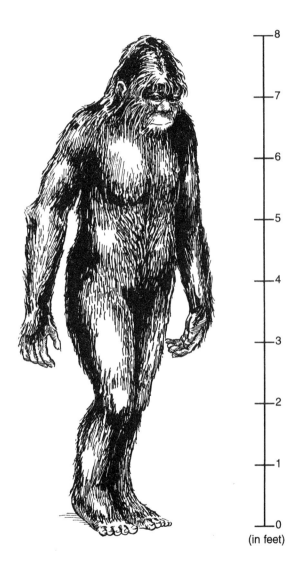

```
— 8

— 7

— 6

— 5

— 4

— 3

— 2

— 1

— 0
(in feet)
```

REGION: *Latin America*	**DESCRIPTIVE INCIDENT:**
CLASS: *Proto-Pygmy*	**DATE:** *1977*
TYPE: *Alux*	**LOCATION:** *Mayapán, Mexico*
DISTINGUISHING CHARACTERISTIC:	**WITNESS:** *Xuc*
long, jet black beard	

Late one night, Xuc, the caretaker of the ruins of the ancient walled city of Mayapán, heard sounds like a machete chopping wood. Xuc opened the entry gate to the site, which is closed to visitors after 5 P.M., and followed the sound, only to be struck by small clay pellets. Peering over a pile of fallen masonry where he had found cover, Xuc saw a tiny man with a disproportionately large head. He had a long, jet black beard and wore a white *huipil,* the Mayan tunic. A long machete was slung over his shoulder.

Until the encounter Xuc regarded tales of the *alux* as mere childhood superstition. But why would someone enter a guarded compound to chop wood when the entire place is surrounded by a vast tropical forest? In answer, Xuc displays some of the hard, baked pellets that he collected from the site the next day. While this is clearly proof of something, it does not explain the puzzling encounter.

But there is a close association between the *alux* and Mayan sites. Located in front of the main temple of many Mayan ruins are tiny stone "houses" with 3-foot-high doorways. Archaeologists say these are "votary shrines," while modern Maya claim they are the homes of the *alux.* Moreover, at some Mayan temples there exist bas-reliefs of pairs of naked little men who are noticeably shorter than the large Mayan priests and the 5-foot-tall Mayan Indian peasants represented in the carvings.

The Maya reported the existence of the *alux* to the first Spanish conquerors. Since then tales and rumors of pygmylike beings—known by various names through many countries, languages and cultural groups—have been especially plentiful from the Yucatán down through the Guianas and Peru, though some reports of these beings extend down to Tierra del Fuego as well. In 1944, for instance, a government timber hunter encountered two little people in the jungles of Honduras. And in 1970 a book published by the Roman Catholic vicariate in Puerto Maldonada, Peru, told of the existence of a tribe of pygmies only 39 inches tall living along the banks of the Curanja River.

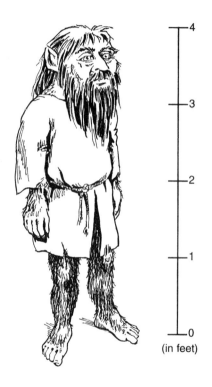

4

3

2

1

0
(in feet)

71

REGION: *Latin America*	**DESCRIPTIVE INCIDENT:**
CLASS: *Proto-Pygmy*	**DATE:** *Mid-1987*
TYPE: *Didi*	**LOCATION:** *Guyana*
DISTINGUISHING CHARACTERISTIC: *"hooing" sounds*	**WITNESS:** *Gary Samuels*

G ary Samuels, a mycologist with the New York Botanical Garden at the time, was scouring the floor of the Guyanese forest, collecting specimens of microfungi that occur on wood. Suddenly he heard footsteps on dry leaves—quite a surprise as he knew that the only other humans in the area were in a camp across the river.

Looking up from the riverbank, Samuels saw what he first assumed was a Guyanese forester about 60 feet away. But the mycologist immediately realized his error: it was actually an apelike creature with brown hair covering its upper body. Samuels could only see the animal from the waist up in the underbrush. In any case, it seemed to be erect, not stooped, and its arms were not dragging on the ground. For a brief moment Samuels wondered whether his partner had perhaps rented out a gorilla costume, but realized that this was unlikely, given their remote location.

The 5-foot-tall "apeman" walked by Samuels in a direct line, as though it had a purpose. The scientist was frightened and was prepared for it to attack. "It was one of those situations where your brain runs through all the possibilities it knows," recalls Samuels, "and comes up with a blank: this was nothing I'd ever seen or heard of before." The thoroughly puzzled Samuels noted that it "moved and sounded like a human, yet it wasn't." It swung its arms at its side as it walked, looking left and right, and making "hoo" noises, as though it was looking for another. When Samuels's partner across the river heard the "hoo" sounds, he assumed they came from Samuels and rowed across to fetch the mycologist.

For hundreds of years, the natives in the Guyanese montane forests from the highlands of Brazil over through Suriname and Guyana have encountered these little "hooing" creatures, whom they generally call *didi*. Sir Walter Raleigh and Laurence Keymis heard rumors of such creatures during their "discovery" of British Guiana (now Guyana) in 1596. Then, in 1769, Dr. Edward Bancroft (Benjamin Franklin's friend and later a British spy in Paris) chronicled stories of what he assumed was a 5-foot-tall ape with short black hair in the area. And in 1910 a British resident magistrate named Haines saw two *didis* along the Konowaruk, near the junction of the Potato River.

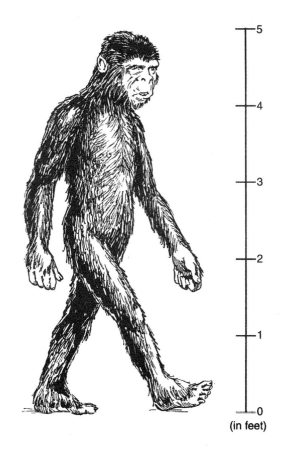

REGION: *Latin America*	**DESCRIPTIVE INCIDENT:**
CLASS: *Unknown Pongid*	DATE: *1930*
TYPE: *Mapinguary*	LOCATION: *Uatumã River, Brazil*
DISTINGUISHING CHARACTERISTIC:	WITNESS: *Inocencio*
bottle-like footprint	

Two days into a ten-man expedition to the source of the Urubú River, a Brazilian hunter, guide, and ferryboat driver named Inocencio became separated from his companions while chasing a troupe of black monkeys. Two hours later, lost and with night falling, Inocencio climbed into a large tree and settled comfortably into a fork between branches. But upon hearing a cry, a "wild and dismal" sound, Inocencio became frightened and loaded his gun. The cry got closer and closer until it sounded "horrible, deafening and inhuman."

Inocencio then heard heavy footfalls as if a large animal was coming closer and closer at top speed. Reaching a fallen tree 40 yards away, the thing let out a grunt and stopped. In the bright starlight, Inocencio could see a silhouette "the size of a man of middle height" that appeared in the clearing. But the "thick-set black figure which stood upright like a man" was no man. When it roared again, Inocencio fired his gun. After another roar and a crash of vegetation, Inocencio saw the beast rushing toward him. He fired again, this time hitting the "terrifying creature," which quickly leapt and hid near the fallen tree but still growled threateningly.

When Inocencio fired again, the black shape roared more loudly and began to retreat. Throughout the night, Inocencio heard its "growl of pain" until at long last it quit, right before dawn. Once down from the tree, Inocencio found blood, crushed leaves, and a "sour penetrating smell." Using the rising sun for orientation, Inocencio quickly found a stream and relocated his companions who were firing off their guns to direct him.

The *mapinguary* is described in native traditions throughout the northern part of Brazil as a mostly red-haired, sloping, bipedal, long-armed giant ape that behaves unpleasantly and leaves unique, bottle-shaped, rounded footprints. Bernard Heuvelmans speculates that an ape with feet adapted to tree dwelling would have very curved toes and be obliged to walk on the outside edge of the foot, leaving just the sort of ringed-shaped prints the *mapinguary* does. Unfortunately, biologist David Oren confused the issue in 1994, when he told *The New York Times* that Amazonian natives were really seeing supposedly extinct giant ground sloths. Though some *mapinguary* sightings may refer to such an animal, others very clearly do not.

5.5
5
4
3
2
1
0
(in feet)

REGION: *Latin America*	**DESCRIPTIVE INCIDENT:**
CLASS: *Giant Monkey*	**DATE:** *1985*
TYPE: *Isnashi, camuenare, makisapa maman*	**LOCATION:** *Southern Ecuador*
DISTINGUISHING CHARACTERISTIC: *black hair*	**WITNESS:** *Benigno Malo*

One day while collecting orchids in the Ecuadorian forests, botanist Benigno Malo was surprised by the sight of a large black "ape" moving through the trees in his direction. The witness managed to snap a photograph of the beast before it disappeared, though efforts by a zoologist at the Natural History Museum in Lima, Peru, to obtain a copy of the photograph have been unsuccessful. Malo basically shrugged the matter off, believing that what he had seen and photographed was nothing more than a circus animal released into the wild.

But Malo's creature bears a strong resemblance to the type of large monkey—still unrecognized by science—that many Peruvian hunters have reported seeing and killing over the past few decades. The creature is generally referred to as the *isnachi*, after the Quechuan word meaning "strong man," though it is also known as *camuenare* ("father of the monkeys") or *makisapa maman* ("mother of the spider monkeys") in other parts of Peru.

Upright, the *isnachi* measures about 4 feet, which is about twice the size of the common spider monkey, *Ateles paniscus*. But the *isnachi* is far more muscular than the lanky and long-armed spider monkey. It has a barrel chest, manlike thighs, and arms that are thicker than those of most men. The *isnachi* is covered with short, thick black hair and has a thick but short tail.

Reports indicate that the *isnachi* lives primarily in tropical forests on isolated ranges between 1,600 and 5,000 feet. According to native hunters, it is only found where wild fruits and *chonta* palms are plentiful; in fact, they state that the presence of dead but standing *chonta* palms is often a good indication of *isnachi* territory. *Isnachi* kills have been reported in the Cerros de Orellana mountain range between the Loreto and San Martin provinces, and in the Cordillera Sira mountain range in the Ucayali province.

The *isnachi* is a solitary creature, only sometimes seen with spider monkeys, though troops of fifteen to twenty have been reported. This Giant Monkey, with a face somewhat resembling a mandrill's, lives in trees. But if angered or threatened it descends quickly, displays a fierce strength, and runs on its hind legs while attacking.

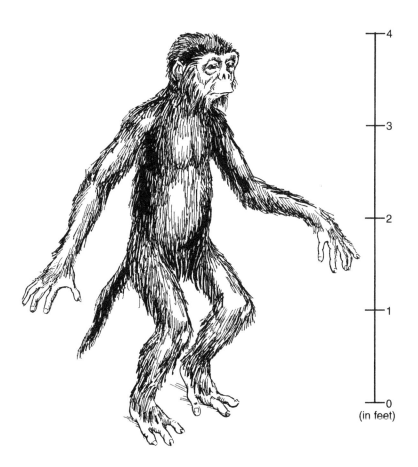

4 —

3 —

2 —

1 —

0 —
(in feet)

REGION: *Latin America*	DESCRIPTIVE INCIDENT:
CLASS: *Giant Monkey*	DATE: *About 1980*
TYPE: *Salvaje*	LOCATION: *Puerto Ayacucho,*
DISTINGUISHING CHARACTERISTIC:	*Venezuela*
red hair	WITNESS: *Fernando Nives*

While hunting 25 miles north of Puerto Ayacucho, a small town on the Orinoco River, Fernando Nives spotted a large monkey, which locals call *salvaje.* As he guided his boat to the shore, the odor from the animal became stronger and stronger. He then noticed that there were three large monkeys on shore. Each one stood more than 5 feet tall and was covered with reddish hair.

During an expedition to Venezuela in 1990, Marc and Khryztian Miller unearthed this and other remarkably similar giant monkey reports. Five years earlier another resident of Puerto Ayacucho reported hearing the call of the *salvaje* when he stopped the bulldozer he was using to clear the area for a new road. A while later, he, too, saw a 5-foot-tall creature with red hair.

At a small village on the Orinoco River, the researchers met an Indian chief who had seen the *salvaje* just a few months earlier. He had been hunting with his blow gun when he saw the 5-foot-tall creature with red hair. The chief shot and killed the giant monkey but did not bring it back to the village, fearing it would be an evil omen.

Many Indian villagers and townspeople of the Venezuelan rain forest have seen the *salvaje,* which has a thin stature and long arms. They have heard its cries and yells, which they describe as humanlike. And they have found its tracks. One well-known jungle pilot found footprints of the *salvaje* on his airstrip in 1988. He reported that the prints were turned inward and estimated that the animal weighed about 80 to 100 pounds. But chances of ever finding this mystery primate in Venezuela's vast and nearly impenetrable forest are, at best, slim.

5
4
3
2
1
0
(in feet)

REGION: *Latin America*	**DESCRIPTIVE INCIDENT:**
CLASS: *Merbeing (freshwater)*	**DATE:** *August 1995*
TYPE: *Chupacabras, Goat Sucker*	**LOCATION:** *Canóvanas, Puerto Rico*
DISTINGUISHING CHARACTERISTIC: *short gray fur with "spikes"*	**WITNESSES:** *Madelyne Tolentino and others*

Sometime during the second week of August, at about four in the afternoon, Madelyne Tolentino noticed that the driver of a vehicle that had pulled up in front of her house appeared frightened. When she approached the large front window to get a better look she saw a creature walking upright in front of her house with its arms outstretched. It walked in an odd, slow, robotic way, as if land was not its primary habitat.

The creature, which eventually became known as the *chupacabras,* meaning "goat sucker" in Spanish, is described as being about 4 feet tall. Its body is covered with short, fine gray fur with darkened spots, perhaps its pink-purplish skin. Its legs are long and skinny and its feet look like those of a goose with three separate toes. It has long, thin arms and hands with three long, skinny fingers with claws. A series of protruding "spikes" runs down its spine.

The face of the *chupacabras* is striking. It has two little holes for a nose and its mouth is little more than a slash. The creature's eyes protrude and run up to its temples and spread to the sides. They look damp and dark and have no whites to them. It's the sight of those eyes that brought a scream to Tolentino's lips: "My God!" Her mother heard this and went outside to chase the creature, which took off in a hopping motion toward the nearby woods. A boy who works for Tolentino's husband in the machine shop across the street put on gloves and actually managed to grab the creature momentarily. A frightened kid on a bicycle started throwing bottles at the *chupacabras.* Tolentino later learned that her husband had seen the same creature in the morning, and that evening two church bus drivers also saw it.

Reports of the *chupacabras* emerged in Puerto Rico in 1995, then spread to the United States, Central America, Brazil, and even Spain in 1996. Like the potto—a type of African primate called a loris that has spikes on its back, tears up small birds, and eats all kinds of meat—the *chupacabras* has very dangerous teeth that favors its reported carnivorous habits. The creature has been blamed for the mutilation and death of numerous goats, sheep, and other animals. Authorities explain the sightings and sequels as being due to feral dogs, parasites, and wild apes—the existence of which would be as remarkable as *chupacabras,* as there are not supposed to be any apes in Latin America.

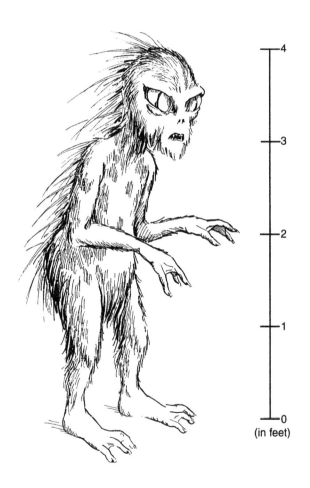

4

3

2

1

0
(in feet)

REGION: *Latin America*
CLASS: *Merbeings (freshwater)*
TYPE: *Negroes-of-the-Water Hairy Dwarf*
DISTINGUISHING CHARACTERISTIC: *webbed feet and hands*

DESCRIPTIVE INCIDENT:
DATE: *May 31, 1985*
LOCATION: *Roque Saenz Peña, Argentina*
WITNESSES: *Luis Galvan, Oscar Aguirre, Carlos Silva, Hector Maidana, Fabian Oviedo, Susana Cladera, Fernando Valenzuela, and others*

On the day in question, Galvan, eleven, and Aguirre, seven, were playing at dusk near an old house when they spotted a 2.5-foot-tall black being. The thing tried to kidnap a five-year-old. There were other sightings in the days to come.

On June 2, Silva, thirteen, was out walking with friends when he saw what they first thought was a monkey in a tree. They said it was humanlike, black, hairy, and dirty with long teeth and big eyes. Two days later, Maidana, twenty-two, was on his way home when he saw a "little black man." The next night, at 9:30, Oviedo, sixteen, saw a "little black man" sitting on a mound, who then ran away. About a half hour later, two other children, Cladera and Valenzuela, saw a little creature appear from behind a car, then run away. They said it was clearly visible in the gaslight.

These recent sightings from Argentina appear to merge with the local native traditions and folklore of what they call "Negroes-of-the-Water." Shorter than humans, they are described as black, bald, amphibious beings with webbed hands and feet. They appear in moonlight and at dusk, thus sharing the mostly nocturnal habits displayed in the 1985 incidents.

Researcher Fabio Picasso notes that these creatures are generally aggressive, "as they often overturn canoes and fisherman's boats. The Negroes-of-the-Water emerge and then soon submerge." Reports of these creatures come from Argentina, Paraguay, and southern Brazil.

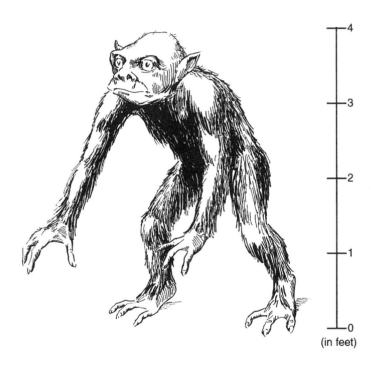

(in feet)

EUROPE

REGION: *Europe*	DESCRIPTIVE INCIDENT:
CLASS: *True Giant*	DATE: *Around A.D. 550*
TYPE: *Grendel*	LOCATION: *Denmark*
DISTINGUISHING CHARACTERISTIC: *matted, reed-covered hair*	WITNESSES: *Beowulf, Hrothgar, and his warriors*

N ight after night a swamp-dwelling, reed-covered, ugly, hairy giant called Grendel would visit Meduseld, the great hall of Hrothgar, who was king of the Danes. Over a period of twelve years, Grendel would repeatedly come in, snatch up one or two of Hrothgar's followers, take them away, and eat them.

Beowulf—son of Ecgtheow and nephew of Hygelac, king of the Geats, whose kingdom was what is now southern Sweden, and later king of the Geats himself—heard from mariners of Grendel's murderous visits and decided to sail from Geatland with fourteen stalwart companions to help Hrothgar. One night after the king and his court had retired and only Beowulf was awake, Grendel entered. With a single stroke Grendel killed one of Beowulf's sleeping men, but Beowulf, unarmed, wrestled with the monster and by dint of his great strength managed to tear Grendel's arm out at the shoulder. Grendel, mortally wounded, retreated, leaving a bloody trail from the hall to his lair.

Later, Grendel's mother, a haglike monster dwelling in a cave at the bottom of a mere (a large swampy pond), returned to avenge her son's death, but Beowulf eventually killed her also.

An English poet told this story well over a thousand years ago. *Beowulf* is the earliest extant poem in a modern European language. It is also the first to mention such a creature. While many may caution against viewing the Grendel story as an actual record of an encounter with a True Giant and his kin, the places and events described in the story are real. This has led various researchers to think that the idea for Grendel might have come from a real creature, regardless of the probably fictional story that was constructed around it. Besides, tales of giants in Europe are known from the time of the Vikings, and according to biologist Ivan T. Sanderson, they persist to the present in reports from the Finnish-Russian border.

12
11
10
9
8
7
6
5
4
3
2
1
0
(in feet)

87

REGION: *Europe*
CLASS: *True Giant*
TYPE: *Big Grey Man, ferla mohr, brenin llwyd*
DISTINGUISHING CHARACTERISTIC: *gray-brown hair*

DESCRIPTIVE INCIDENT:
DATE: *January pre-1952*
LOCATION: *Ben MacDhui, Scotland*
WITNESS: *Unnamed*

A t 4,296 feet, Ben MacDhui is the tallest peak in the Cairngorm Mountain range in central Scotland. One day the witness, a friend of the mountaineer Richard Frere (who relates the story), decided to spend a night alone near the large cairn on the summit of Ben Mac-Dhui. Suddenly, a huge creature came "swaggering" down the hill just 20 or so yards away from the witness.

The creature, which rolled slightly from side to side as it took its huge measured steps, was easily 20 feet high and covered with short brown hair. Its head, which was disproportionately large, was set atop a thick, apparently powerful neck. The giant had very wide shoulders, relatively slim hips, and stood extremely erect. Though its hairy arms were long, it did not resemble an ape.

Many reputable climbers have reported hearing strange footsteps on this mountain. While descending the summit in 1891, professor Norman Collie heard one crunch after another in the mist, "as if someone was walking after me but taking steps three or four times the length of my own."

An experienced climber named Tom Crowley also saw a giant on Braeraich, near Ben MacDhui, in the early 1920s. Hearing footsteps, Crowley looked behind and saw a huge gray figure. The misty figure, known locally as the *ferla mohr*, appeared to have pointed ears, long legs, and feet that bore talons rather than toes. Terrified by this sight, Crowley fled to the glen below. While Crowley reported a gray creature and others have said it was brown, the apparent discrepancy may be due to lighting differences. And the "talons" Crowley reported might simply be long toenails.

Legends of giants can be found throughout the British Isles. *Brenin Ilwyd* is the name of a powerful legendary being from the northern mountains of Wales. This "grey king" or "monarch of the mist" apparently stole children and adults who ventured unwarily into the misty heights. Some researchers wonder if the legend might not be a memory of a Big Grey Man-type figure.

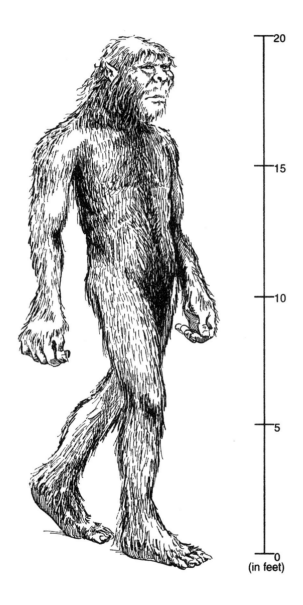

20

15

10

5

0
(in feet)

89

REGION: *Europe*	DESCRIPTIVE INCIDENT:
CLASS: *Neandertaloid*	DATE: *1870*
TYPE: *Wudewasa, se'ir*	LOCATION: *Bilogora, Croatia*
DISTINGUISHING CHARACTERISTIC:	WITNESSES: *Two brothers, unnamed*
prominent brow ridges	

During the cold winter, the two brothers slept together in a warm stable. In the middle of one night, one brother awoke when he felt as if there was someone between the two of them. When he touched it, it felt hairy and warm, and at first he thought it was their dog. Then slightly brushing against a breast made him realize that it was female. Suddenly frightened, he called his brother. The hairy female quickly made for the door and the two brothers followed her out into the courtyard. She was quicker than they were, however, and jumped over the fence to the garden and on into the woods.

The deep snow forced the brothers to give up their chase, but they saw the woman quite clearly in the moonlight. It was a *wudewasa*, one of the hairy beings "somewhat lower than humans" who lived in the woods. Later, when they told their father about the incident, he expressed little surprise; it was common for them to warm themselves beside humans during cold winters, he explained.

The short-statured *wudewasa* wore no clothes, as they were covered with long, thick hair. They had short hair on their heads and fringe beards under their chins. Their naked faces showed a prominent brow ridge, a large nose, full and wide mouth, and deep-set eyes. They had short legs and long arms, but their hands and feet were clearly hominid. Though generally timid, they sometimes ventured into human territory when either cold or hungry.

Researchers suspect these creatures were the Satyrs of classical antiquity—a name borrowed from the Hebrew *se'ir,* meaning "hairy one." In the Middle Ages they acquired the name *wudewasa*, or "wood being." Ireland saw reports of the *wudewasa* until the thirteenth century and people of the Pyrenees and Carpathians saw them until the eighteenth century. If they survive at all in modern Europe, they are most likely to be found in the montane forests of northern Scandinavia, where some country folk assert the *wudewasa* still exist.

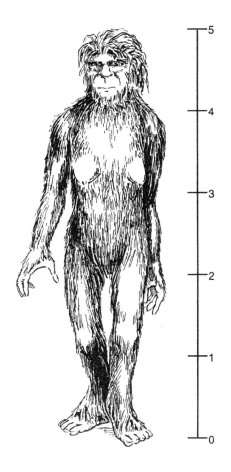

REGION: *Europe*
CLASS: *Erectus Hominid*
TYPE: *Kaptar, biabin-guli*
DISTINGUISHING CHARACTERISTIC:
animal-like eyes in a protruding face

DESCRIPTIVE INCIDENT:
DATE: *Late fall 1941*
LOCATION: *Caucasus Mountains,
Buinaksk, Daghestan*
WITNESS: *Lt. Col. V. S. Karapetyan*

K arapetyan, an officer in the Medical Service of the Soviet Army, was asked by Buinaksk villagers to examine a *kaptar*, or *biabin-guli*, they had captured in the nearby mountains. They wanted to know if the beast was a disguised spy. Taken into a cold shed where the "man" was being held (because he had sweated profusely inside a house), Karapetyan saw a male, naked and barefoot. He was about 6 feet tall but appeared "like a giant" to Karapetyan, who noticed that his eyes were "dull and empty—those of an animal," and his fingers were thick, strong, and exceptionally large.

The *kaptar* was extremely hairy. His human-shaped chest, back, and shoulders were covered with shaggy, dark brown hair. The fur was "like that of a bear" and about 1 inch long, but below the chest, it was softer and thinner. The wrists were sparsely covered with hair, while the palms of the hands and soles of the feet were completely free of hair. Long, rough head hair reached his shoulders. Karapetyan noticed that although his face was completely covered with a light growth of hair, he had no moustache or beard. Karapetyan gave his opinion that this was not a spy in disguise, but a wildman. He would hear, years later, that the *kaptar* had been killed.

Kaptar have frequently been seen in the Caucasus during the past forty years. Hunters say the *kaptar* are usually covered by brown hair, stand 5 to 6 feet tall, and have an ugly protruding face but are upright, strong and agile. They leave large, broad, humanlike footprints.

Several Soviet and post-Soviet expeditions have searched for these montane hominids. Marie-Jeanne Koffmann, a French-Russian surgeon, has lived on and off in the Caucasus since 1959 and has interviewed over four thousand local eyewitnesses. While some associate the *kaptar* with the desert-dwelling, smaller *almas* of eastern Asia, these creatures are clearly different, being mountain inhabitants of the Caucasus range found to the south and west of the Urals. Most Russian and French scientists working on the *kaptar* feel they may be examples of surviving Neandertals. But others, noting their lack of a beaky nose, and a much more protohuman physique, disagree.

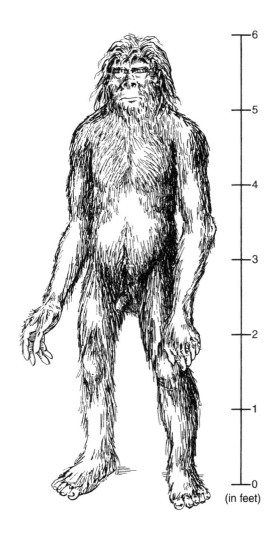

6

5

4

3

2

1

0
(in feet)

REGION: *Europe*	**DESCRIPTIVE INCIDENT:**
CLASS: *Merbeing (marine)*	**DATE:** *May 1817*
TYPE: *Mermen*	**LOCATION:** *Atlantic Ocean*
DISTINGUISHING CHARACTERISTIC: *white belly*	**WITNESSES:** *Second Mate Stevens and crew*

In 1820 the *American Journal of Science* published a curious extract from the logbook of the ship *Leonidas*. At two in the afternoon, the ship was just off the coast of France when the crew spotted a "strange fish" about half a ship's length away. Though its lower portion resembled a fish, from the breast up it looked like a human being. Its belly was white and the top of its back was brown. The creature had short hair to the top of its head.

The crew observed the Merman's motions and shape over the span of six hours. While close to the ship, he would stand erect out of the water about two feet, looking back at the ship's observers "earnestly," according to the log. Then he would dive and reappear on the other side of the ship.

Second Mate Stevens said the creature had a very human-like, nearly white face and black hair on his head. His arms were only half as long as the second mate's but his hands were humanlike. From head to tail, the Merman measured about 5 feet.

Reports of Mermaids and Mermen are deeply embedded in European legend and lore. But in Scotland in the early nineteenth century they emerged into everyday life. A Mermaid with long green hair was seen off northeastern Scotland on January 12, 1809. Then in the summer of 1814 more sightings of a half-human, half-fish creature occurred off Scotland's west coast.

Two independent witnesses reported seeing a creature with a humanlike, all-white upper half and a seemingly scaly brown bottom half sitting on a black rock on the seacoast of Corphine in Kintyre on October 13, 1822. The creature was 4 to 5 feet long and had short arms and long hair. The creature finally tumbled into the water and disappeared.

Sightings of Merfolk in the seas off Scotland have continued into the twentieth century. Fishermen off Craig More reported such a creature as recently as August 1949. Notably the Merfolk of experience are manifestly different from those of superstition, which sport golden hair, supernatural powers, and the ability to speak with humans. The abundance and persistence of these reports can only be explained by the existence of an as yet unrecognized species of dugong, manatee, or sea cow—or an unknown form of primate adapted to sea life.

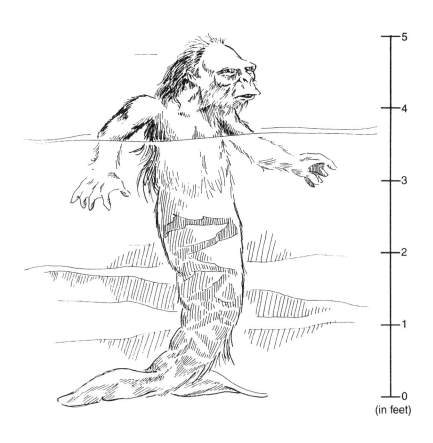

5

4

3

2

1

0
(in feet)

AFRICA

REGION: *Africa*	**DESCRIPTIVE INCIDENT:**
CLASS: *True Giant*	**DATE:** *Pre-1911*
TYPE: *Tano Giant*	**LOCATION:** *Upper Tano, Gold Coast*
DISTINGUISHING CHARACTERISTIC:	**WITNESSES:** *Unnamed*
light skin under black hair	

On several occasions the male hunters and women of a village near the primeval forests of the Upper Tano were terrified by "a white ape of extraordinary stature." With arms described as being as thick as a man's body, the creature must indeed have been "past all man" in size. The wildman of the woods was said to have white skin with black hair growing through it. Its head was flat and about the size of a large monkey's. Big teeth stuck out of its monkeylike mouth, and its hands had four fingers but no thumb, yet it was said to carry around the skin of a "bush cow," which it wrapped itself up in when cold.

The villagers feared the Tano Giant's voracious appetite. They barricaded their doors at night and on jungle paths they left broiled plantain and cassava. It is said to have once carried off a woman, who never returned, and supposedly took several children as well, whose bodies were later found mutilated and disemboweled—but not mutilated the way a leopard does, the West Africans were quick to note. Once the fierce giant supposedly broke the gun of a hunter who tried to shoot him. The only thing that made this wildman run away, according to the villagers, was fire.

There are two novel aspects to this account. One is the light skin covered with black hairs. The other is the absence of a thumb. But perhaps its thumb was simply small relative to the rest of its hand—like the thumb of the *Plesianthropus,* as one researcher pointed out—and carried pressed against the side of the palm so that it would not be easily visible.

The naturalist Ivan T. Sanderson, who got to know the West Africans well and fully appreciated their storytelling abilities, found them quite straightforward when it came to questions of their native fauna. Despite the unique nature of this being, however, Sanderson thought that the accounts of this creature, which were not told as traditional tales, carried some validity.

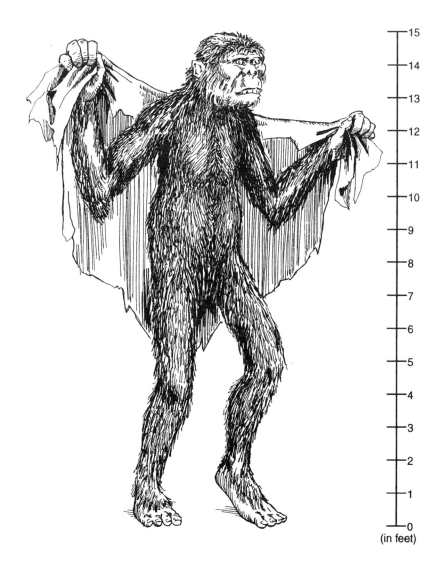

15
14
13
12
11
10
9
8
7
6
5
4
3
2
1
0
(in feet)

REGION: *Africa*	**DESCRIPTIVE INCIDENT:**
CLASS: *Proto-Pygmy*	**DATE:** *1906*
TYPE: *Kakundakári, agogwe, séhité*	**LOCATION:** *Walikalé, Belgian Congo*
DISTINGUISHING CHARACTERISTIC:	*(now Zimbabwe)*
flat nose	**WITNESS:** *Unnamed*

While among the Warega in 1956, the Belgian herpetologist Paul Leloup heard a remarkably detailed account of the little man of the great forest, the *kakundakári*. The story came from a sixty-year-old man whose father, fifty years previously, had actually killed one of these creatures.

One day while walking beside a stream the father had heard a slight noise. Carefully seeking out the source of the noise he came upon a squatting *kakundakári*, who was overturning rocks and feeding off tiny crabs. Taking aim, the father threw his javelin and pierced the creature's stomach. That night, when he brought the corpse back to the village, everyone recognized it immediately as a *kakundakári*. In the days that followed, many came from neighboring villages to see the rare creature.

The son, who saw the *kakundakári* himself, identified it as a female. She was about 3 feet tall, black skinned, and covered with short gray hairs, except on her head, where the hair was long and black. Her face was humanlike with a large forehead, though her nose was flat. She had small ears and a large mouth, somewhat like a chimpanzee's, though her teeth were humanlike, without large canines. Her hands were also like a human's but the big toes of her feet angled off to the side.

Reports suggest that these primitive, hairy, long-haired beings are cave dwellers. They vary in height from about 2 to 4 feet. Their feet measure about 5 inches and they have four toes, the little toe being atrophied. Their big toes are slightly angled and proportionally longer than those of humans.

These creatures are known by a variety of names throughout Africa. In Central Africa, they may also be called *amajungi* or *niaka-ambuguza*; in East Africa as *agogwe, doko, mau,* or *mberikimo*; in Southern Africa as *chimanimani* or *tokoleshe,* and in West Africa as *abonesi, ijiméré,* or *séhité.* In the 1940s, there were numerous reports of reddish-haired *séhité* in the Ivory Coast, where there were no known pygmies at all. Bernard Heuvelmans believes these small creatures may be either Proto-Pygmies, proto-bushmen, or surviving australopithecines (gracile species). Heuvelmans comments: "Now there is no known ape, even among the anthropoids, which normally walks upright on its hind legs. . . . Perhaps [they] are therefore really little men."

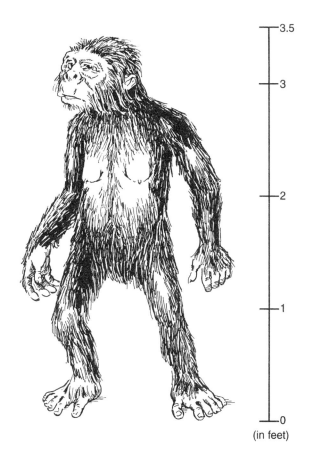

3.5

3

2

1

0
(in feet)

101

REGION: *Africa*	DESCRIPTIVE INCIDENT:
CLASS: *Unknown Pongid*	DATE: *Pre-1917*
TYPE: *Ngoloko, muhalu, kikomba*	LOCATION: *Witu District, Kenya*
DISTINGUISHING CHARACTERISTIC: *elephant-like ears*	WITNESSES: *Heri wa Mabruko and unnamed others*

O ne day Heri wa Mabruko, some Swahili friends, and an Mboni bushman were tapping rubber trees in the forest. While busy at work, the bushman spotted a *ngoloko* stalking the group. The bushman then fired off an arrow that struck the creature. As the *ngoloko* ran off, the men followed, only to find it lying outstretched on the ground, some 500 yards away from where it had been hit.

The *ngoloko* was still breathing and smelled awful. The creature measured 8 feet from head-to-toe and was a male. His body was the size of two men and covered with lots of long, thick gray hair. So long was the hair on his head and upper body, in fact, that a single strand of hair measured 3 feet in length.

But his dark-skinned face, which featured a prominent nose with two nostrils, was hairless. It had a relatively small mouth and big teeth. Most striking were his big flapping ears, which resembled an elephant's. The creature's chin and low forehead were both retreating. His eyes were large with eyelashes joined to the hair around the face.

The witnesses had all the time in the world to observe the dying creature. His hands each had one finger, which ended in a single hooked claw 2.5 to 3 inches long and a thumb. His feet had a very large prehensile thumb and three toes, one ending in a great claw.

J. A. G. Elliot, who recorded this account in his 1934 book, *Tales of Africa,* also heard the creature's distinctive cry (more frightening than a gorilla's) and studied its tracks while traveling through the Wa-Sanje, a land of lagoons, mangrove swamps, and bush along the coast. From one particularly impressive set of footprints he concluded that the animal was a biped and had a stride ranging from 1.5 feet (walking) to 9 feet (running).

In the Congo these 8-foot-tall creatures with very long head hair and large prehensile toes are known variously as *muhalu* or as *kikomba*. But no large flapping ears were reported, as in the Kenya accounts; perhaps the ears were hidden by the long head hair. The last reliable reports of these giant apelike creatures date back to the early 1960s.

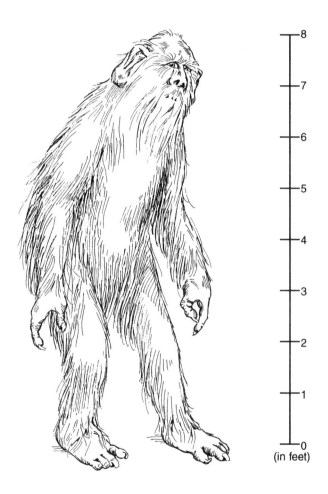

8

7

6

5

4

3

2

1

0
(in feet)

REGION: *Africa*	DESCRIPTIVE INCIDENT:
CLASS: *Giant Monkey*	DATE: *March 8, 1913*
TYPE: *Nandi Bear, chemosit, kodoelo*	LOCATION: *Mile 16, Magadi Railway, East Africa*
DISTINGUISHING CHARACTERISTIC: *high withers*	WITNESS: *Hickes*

H ickes, an engineer in charge of building the Magadi Railway, was traveling along on a motor trolley at 25 mph when he spotted what first appeared to be a hyena about 50 yards ahead. Though the "hyena" had seen Hickes and was heading off-line at a right angle, the trolley approached faster than the animal could escape through the 18-inch-high grass.

Hickes wondered what a "hyena" was doing out at nine in the morning, then realized that it was not a hyena. The animal was about as tall as a lion and tawny in color. Its thickset body had high withers and a broad rump. The animal had a short neck, stumpy nose, and very short ears. As it ran off with its forelegs and both hind legs rising at the same time, Hickes noted that its very shaggy hair reached right down to its feet, which were large and covered with black mud.

Once past, Hickes realized that what he had seen was the strange beast that many had either heard of or reported seeing during the railway's construction. Several engineers originally had spotted a strange footprint in the mud that resembled a bear's. Then a native servant had seen such an animal standing on its hind legs. Subsequently a subcontractor had seen an animal resembling the Hickes creature. Accounts often mentioned a thick mane, long claws, large teeth, and an upright stance of 6 feet.

Hickes's account, which was collected by the anthropologist C. W. Hobley, is but a small part of this strange beast's rather confusing history. What the local people, the Nandi, had long called the *chemosit*, the British named the Nandi Bear because of its footprint and tendency to rise up on its hind legs. There is, however, not a single species of bear in all of sub-Saharan Africa. Mixed into reports of this beast are also sightings of what may be a giant African ratel or large black honey badgers, as well as the savage deeds of spotted hyenas of unusual size or color.

The Wa-Pokomo call this creature the *kodoelo* and describe it as an enormous baboon. Bernard Heuvelmans notes that some Nandi Bear reports may relate to the fossil finds of the giant baboon *Dinopithecus* of Africa.

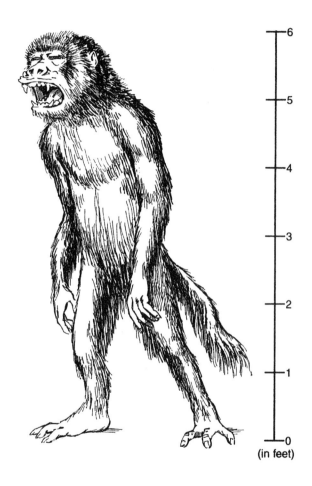

6

5

4

3

2

1

0
(in feet)

REGION: *Africa*	DESCRIPTIVE INCIDENT:
CLASS: *Merbeing (freshwater)*	DATE: *Pre-1950*
TYPE: *Kalanoro*	LOCATION: *Madagascar*
DISTINGUISHING CHARACTERISTIC:	WITNESSES: *Sakalava and Bara people*
three toes	

The *kalanoro* are similar to our own gnomes and elves but all the tribes of Madagascar believe in them, according to Raymond Decary, who in the 1950s researched the common themes connecting the stories of the *kalanoro*.

Some tribes see the *kalanoro* as amphibious creatures. Around Lake Aloatra, they are thought to be females who live at the bottom of the water and have hair that falls to their waist, like *naiads* or Mermaids. But around Lake Kinkony, the Sakalava tribe regards the *kalanoro* as males who live in the thickets and reeds on the edges of lagoons. They are said to be less than 3 feet high, have sweet female voices, and possess but three toes on each foot. They supposedly live on fish and raw food, and lead humans astray.

Other tribes, however, regard the *kalanoro* as a land dweller. The Betsileo tribe, for instance, thinks the *kalanoro* is a little female land dwarf, not more than 2 feet high and covered with hair. In northern Madagascar the *kalanoro* are thought to live in woods and caves and have hooked nails that inflict cruel wounds on all who try to capture them. And to the Bara tribe, the *kalanoro* are quick and nimble little forest dwellers with long hair who reside in the Ankazoabo district and come out at night to search the villages for food.

These "legends may be fantastic," wrote Bernard Heuvelmans in 1955, but "they are found all over Madagascar, and it would be odd if they were utterly without foundation," especially given the fact that "some areas of Madagascar are still almost unexplored, such as the Ambongo reserve and the lonely Isalo mountains, and there are still some 3 or 4 million hectares of virgin forest." These reports of the amphibious, long-haired, three-toed *kalanoro* also match remarkably well other reports of Merbeings from around the world.

3

2

1

0
(in feet)

ASIA

REGION: *Asia*	**DESCRIPTIVE INCIDENT:**
CLASS: *Neo-Giant*	**DATE:** *Late March 1942*
TYPE: *Gin-sung, Big Yeti*	**LOCATION:** *Chumbi Valley, Tibet*
DISTINGUISHING CHARACTERISTIC:	**WITNESSES:** *Slavomir Rawicz, Anton*
square head	*Paluchowicz, Eugene Zaro, Anastazi*
	Kolemenos, and Mr. Smith

During World War II, seven inmates slipped out of a Siberian labor camp and began a four thousand-mile escape to India. The 1956 book *The Long Walk* tells of this incredible trek to freedom and includes a firsthand account by Slavomir Rawicz of an encounter with a pair of what they called "Abominable Snowmen."

There were just five survivors as the men neared the end of their journey, in the foothills of the Himalayas near the border with India. While descending a large mountain, they saw "two moving black specks" in the snowfield below them, about a quarter mile away. As they approached and reached the edge of a bluff, Rawicz and his companions found they were just 12 feet above and 100 yards away from the beasts.

"They were enormous and they walked on their hind legs," Rawicz wrote. Using his military training, he estimated the animals were not much under 8 feet high, though one was a few inches shorter than the other. Their shoulders "sloped down to a powerful chest" and their long arms had wrists reaching to the knees. Their heads were squarish and from the back had a straight line from the crown into the shoulders. The reddish appearance of the beasts came from their rusty brown hair, which formed a tight, close fur against their bodies, but this was intermingled with "long, loose, straight hairs, hanging downwards, which has a slight greyish tinge. . . ."

The beasts shuffled around and turned toward the men occasionally, though obviously they were unconcerned. After two hours of observation, however, the five men decided they had to push on and took a path that avoided the creatures, which looked "strong enough to eat us."

Their description of the creatures fits stories of the typical Big Yeti from the northern area of the Himalayas and the *gin-sung* ("bear-men") of China. One typical track of the beast, found during the Slick-Johnson Snowman Expedition of 1958, shows a 13-inch hominid print with all five toes pointing forward. Bernard Heuvelmans notes that reports of these bigger sized Yetis agree on the animals being dark in color and found in Tibet or in the very north of Sikkim and Nepal.

8

7

6

5

4

3

2

1

0
(in feet)

111

REGION: *Asia*
CLASS: *True Giant*
TYPE: *Nyalmo, orang dalam*
DISTINGUISHING CHARACTERISTIC:
two-foot-long, four-toed footprints

DESCRIPTIVE INCIDENT:
DATE: *Pre-1937*
LOCATION: *Northern Nepal*
WITNESS: *Unnamed*

A well-educated Indian pilgrim was visiting Tibetan monasteries on the northern frontier of Nepal, when Nepalese friends told him of an armed expedition setting out in search of giant snowmen who spoke an unknown language. The pilgrim decided to join them; the group walked through forests for eight days before encountering their prize. But when they heard a rumbling and came across an enormous set of tracks, each about 2 feet long in the moist clay, all but three members of the terrified party decided to turn back.

Proceeding cautiously, the pilgrim and two others then stumbled upon a "remarkable spectacle." Among the high rocks, they beheld a circle of "giant ape-men" 10 to 13 feet tall. One was banging a drum made from a hollow tree trunk, while the others swayed to the beat. To the pilgrim, the gathering smacked of religious ritual.

Despite the bitter cold, the giants were naked, warmed only by the hair that covered their bodies. The pilgrim noted a "strange sadness" in their faces; their features were a cross between gorilla and human. Yet "there was nothing of the animal in their attitude," according to the witness.

The Tibetan mountain people called these giants *nyalmo.* Some are said to measure 20 feet tall. A report from 1957 suggests that the *nyalmo* have conical heads, usually wander about in groups in the snowy terrain above 12,000 feet, and are carnivorous and man-eating. The early 1980s produced reports of large footprints, up to 19 inches but with just four toes, from the Gissar Mountains of Tajikistan. The large, four-toes track is characteristic of the True Giant.

The Malay Peninsula has also had its sightings of 20-foot-tall giants, with reports dating back to the 1930s. In 1961 their large four-toes tracks were found in the state of Johore. A decade later, an expedition that set out to find the *orang dalam* ("interior people"), as they are known in Malaysia, failed to reach the plateau at the head of the Endau River, which is said to be their home, but the searchers did find their large footprints. More strange four-toed tracks were reported in Malaysia in January 1995.

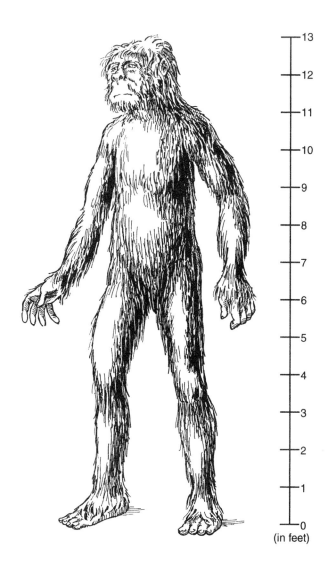

13
12
11
10
9
8
7
6
5
4
3
2
1
0
(in feet)

113

REGION: *Asia*	DESCRIPTIVE INCIDENT:
CLASS: *Marked Hominid*	DATE: *August 16, 1987*
TYPE: *Mecheny, mirygdy*	LOCATION: *Western Siberia*
DISTINGUISHING CHARACTERISTIC:	WITNESSES: *Maya Bykova, Volodya,*
white hair on arm	*and Nadya*

During a train trip in 1985, Maya Bykova met Volodya, an ethnic Mansi, the indigenous people of western Siberia, who told the researcher of repeated visits by a tall, hairy, humanlike creature to the family hunting cabin over a period of forty years. As a rule the creature showed up just before dawn, announcing its arrival by a knock on the window. The sightings invariably occurred during August.

Following an invitation by Volodya and his wife, Nadya, Bykova visited the family cabin, which was set in a cedar forest surrounded by bogs, in August 1987. At dawn the day after their arrival, they heard two quick knocks on the window and all three shot out of bed and dashed out the door. And there, about 15 feet away, was a figure standing with its right shoulder leaning against the bare trunk of a dead cedar.

The manlike animal stood about 6.5 feet tall and was covered with reddish brown hair some 2 to 3 inches long. The only exception was his left forearm, which was covered with white hair. For this reason they called him Mecheny, which translates as the "Marked One." The creature had no visible genitals, long straight legs, and enormous feet. Its arms were hefty and hung loosely forward. The palms of its enormous, scoop like hands were hairless and red.

The creature's head, which was elongated at the back and covered with hair only about an inch long, stood directly on the wide shoulders of its barrel-like chest; the being had no neck. Its eyes were almond-shaped and set deep under a prominent brow ridge; its mouth was a long narrow slit; and its jaw jutted forward slightly.

After about a minute Volodya's dog started barking and the Mecheny turned, stepped behind a tree, and disappeared into the forest. Upon a return visit in October, Volodya and Bylcova found the family dog ripped apart from the tail to the collarbone. The following August, the three again chanced to observe the Mecheny for about an hour. They found it jumping around, falling on the ground occasionally, then standing up, and putting something in its mouth. The witnesses presumed it was feeding on frogs, lizards, or mice.

Mecheny appears to be a specific piebald individual of what the local people call the *mirygdy,* meaning "broad-shoulders."

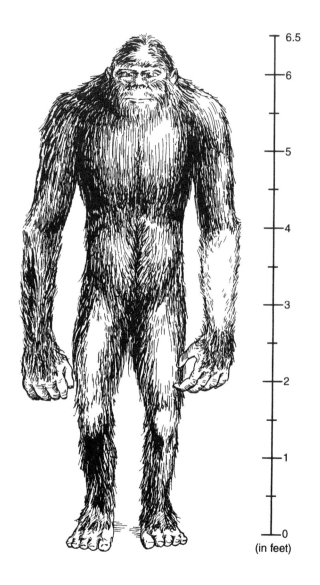

6.5

6

5

4

3

2

1

0
(in feet)

115

REGION: *Asia*	DESCRIPTIVE INCIDENT:
CLASS: *Marked Hominid*	DATE: *1920s*
TYPE: *Chuchunaa, mulen*	LOCATION: *Eastern Siberia*
DISTINGUISHING CHARACTERISTIC:	WITNESSES: *Tatyana Zakharova and*
wears clothes	*others*

Some time after the Russian Revolution, the Tungus reindeer herder Tatyana Zakharova was with a group of people gathering berries in the mountains east of the Yana and Indigirka rivers when they saw a *chuchunaa,* also picking and eating berries. Upon seeing the humans, the *chuchunaa* stood straight up. "He was very tall and lean, say over six feet," remembered Zakharova. "He was dressed in a deer skin, and was barefoot. He had a big face, like a man's but dark. His forehead was small and hung over his eyes like a peaked cap. He had a big chin, broad and much bigger than a man's. All in all he was like a man, but of much greater stature. After a second he ran off. He ran very quickly, leaping high after every third step."

The sightings of the *chuchunaa,* or the *mulen* as it is known in the southern portion of its range, are concentrated in the area of eastern Siberia in the Verkhoyansk and Poloustnaya mountain ranges, specifically among two groups of people, the Tungus and the Yahut. A report to a Communist Party commission on Yahut affairs in 1928 recommended that the party take an interest in the *chuchunaa.* Another report, a year later, this one to the (Soviet Western Siberian) Commission for the Discovery and Study of Natural Antiquarian Curiosities, said the *mulen* and *chuchunaa* should be studied before they became extinct.

"The *chuchunaa's* face is black, and it's hard to make out the nose and the eyes," notes Soviet historian and ethnographer G. V. Ksenofontov. "He lives in a lair like a bear. His voice is unpleasant, grating and hoarse. He whistles, frightening people and reindeer. Men come across him very rarely and often see him running away." While some have theorized that these hominids may be Neandertals, archaeologist Myra Shackley disagrees: ". . . the *chuchunaa,* usually reported to be over 6 ft. 6 in. tall, are really too big for the average Neandertaler (typical height 5 ft. 6 in.)." The *chuchunaa*—an often clothed, eastern version of the *mirygdy*—are a perfect example of the Marked Hominid.

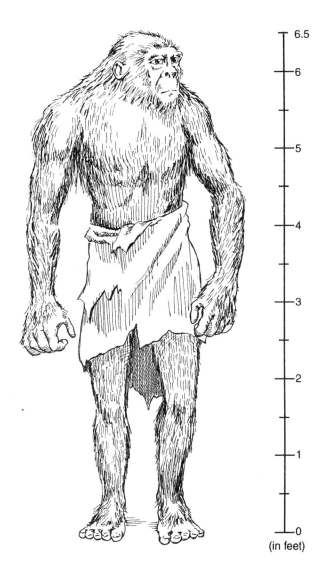

6.5

6

5

4

3

2

1

0

(in feet)

117

REGION: *Asia*	**DESCRIPTIVE INCIDENT:**
CLASS: *Neandertaloid*	**DATE:** *1922*
TYPE: *Chinese Wildman*	**LOCATION:** *Malan, Fangxian, China*
DISTINGUISHING CHARACTERISTIC: *red hair on knees*	**WITNESSES:** *Huan Xinhe, Huang Xinming, Huang Xinkui*

When Huan Xinhe was nine years old, he saw a redhaired Wildman that had been captured. He first saw the creature from inside his house, as dozens of soldiers walked by escorting a Wildman bound with an iron chain. When the soldiers tied it to a tree, Huan Xinhe went out to look at it. "It was two meters tall, and covered with brown hair all over its body," Huan Xinhe recalled five decades later. "The roots of the hair were red. Both its hands and feet were longer than a human's, and so were its fingers and toes. It was strong. I observed it carefully until the soldiers took it away."

Two other witnesses, Huang Xinming and Huang Xinkui, confirmed the story. "The Wildman was so large that it terrified me," recalled Huang Xinming at the age of eighty-one. "Its feet were thirty to forty centimeters long. But the soldiers said it wasn't one of the really big ones. It was covered with dark red hair all over its body. The hair on its feet was paler, and its palms and the soles of its feet were bare."

The other witness, Huang Xinkui, recalled: "The soldiers escorted the Wildman down the mountains with four men carrying a one-meter-high wooden cage. When it moved, they put an iron chain round its neck. When it refused to walk, they put it into the cage and carried it. When it walked, it bent forward and loped."

In another incident, a witness named Fan Jingquan twice saw a pair of Chinese "Wildpeople," while working for a Ministry of Heavy Industry geological prospecting team in northwest China in the 1950s. On consecutive days he briefly spotted what appeared to be a mother and its young in a chestnut grove where the locals claimed the Wildpeople roamed. "She was at least 1.6 meters tall, and had a young one with her," Fan Jingquan recalled. "I could see a blood stain on her leg. The reddish-brown hairs on her knees were undisturbed, so I figured she walked upright at all times and never crawled."

Encounters with Neandertaloids are rare, but incidents such as this and folklore on bipedal, redhaired near-humans can be found in eastern and central Asia.

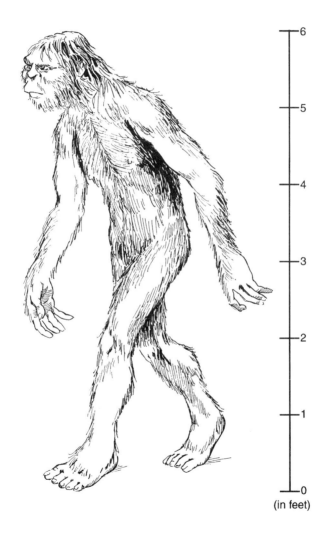

6 —

5 —

4 —

3 —

2 —

1 —

0 —
(in feet)

119

REGION: *Asia*	**DESCRIPTIVE INCIDENT:**
CLASS: *Erectus Hominid*	**DATE:** *1963*
TYPE: *Almas*	**LOCATION:** *Altai Mountains, Mongolia*
DISTINGUISHING CHARACTERISTIC: *bare, callused knees*	**WITNESS:** *Ivan Ivlov*

Ivan Ivlov, a Russian children's doctor with an excellent reputation, was traveling through southern Mongolia when he spotted what appeared to be a family of manlike creatures standing on a mountain slope. Using a pair of field glasses, Ivlov saw what looked like a male, female, and small child about half a mile away. Ivlov and his Mongolian driver observed the "family" for some time, until finally the three creatures disappeared behind a jutting rock. The driver told Ivlov that these creatures were common in the area. Though once a skeptic, Ivlov decided to interview his children patients in the area to see if they had seen such creatures—and indeed, many had.

Adult *almas* are 5 to 6 feet tall and covered in reddish black hair, except for their faces and hands, which are hairless, and their abdomens, which are only sparsely covered. *Almas,* have a flattened forehead, prominent browridge, protruding jaw, and cone-shaped back of the head. They have broad shoulders and long arms and walk with bent knees, which are always bare. Females have long breasts.

Almas are usually observed at dawn and at dusk. They lead reclusive, nocturnal lives, and are timid and easily frightened. They feed primarily on roots, leaves, grass, and other vegetation. They have been seen to use simple tools, but have not been heard to speak.

Almas means "wildman," or a cross between man and ape, in the Mongolian language. The *almas* are said to live in the Altai mountains in western Mongolia and in the Tien Shan Mountains of nearby Sinkiang in China. The earliest known printed reference to the *almas* dates back to the fifteenth century with a sighting by Hans Schiltberger, a nobleman from Bavaria. In the late eighteenth century a manuscript on natural history treated the *almas* as one of the region's local animals. Sightings decreased in the nineteenth century, perhaps due to the encroachment of civilization. Nevertheless, modern accounts continue. Members of the Mongolian Academy of Sciences collected many eyewitness sightings during the last half of the twentieth century. One eighteen-month expedition headed by Ravjir saw footprints of the *almas* in snow on December 15, 1973. They followed the tracks for 16 miles over two days, before the prints disappeared in the Yolt Mountains.

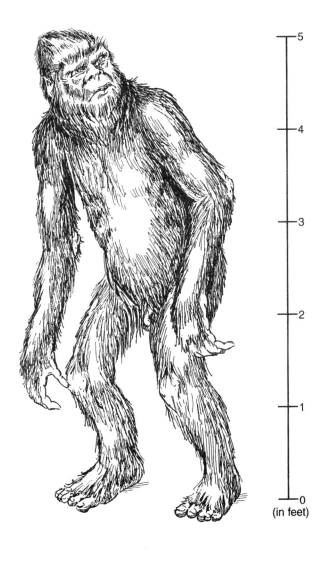

5

4

3

2

1

0
(in feet)

121

REGION: *Asia*	DESCRIPTIVE INCIDENT:
CLASS: *Erectus Hominid*	DATE: *1971*
TYPE: *Nguoi rung, Vietnamese Forest People*	LOCATION: *Ae Thi, Dak Lak, Vietnam*
	WITNESS: *Recom Hiun*
DISTINGUISHING CHARACTERISTIC: *stubby, upturned nose*	

The Ai Thi tribespeople of this mountain village regularly went fishing in faraway forest streams to the south. But during one stretch of time they were puzzled why their fish traps were all without fish. Then one day they discovered a footprint one and a half times as large as a normal human footprint near a trap. So they set up an ambush.

Several nights later, just before dawn, two apelike creatures came strolling out of the forest. One, a female, was slightly shorter than the other, a male. They were both slim creatures, their bodies covered with long hair. Fur covered their faces but not their palms or soles.

When the male tipped over one of the fish traps, the men ambushed the pair, tied them up, and took them back to their village. Word of the event spread quickly and a team of scientists from Duc My brought along some South Korean soldiers, who were there because of the war, to examine the captives. Recom Hiun, then director of the Department for the Development of Ethnic Minorities of Khanh Hoa province, was also there and witnessed what happened next.

The soldier proceeded to shave the facial hair of the apelike captives, who had been bound to two house posts with ropes. The couple was then washed, dressed, and spirited away by the South Koreans to their base at Duc My. No one knows what happened afterward.

These bipedal, 6-foot-tall creatures with stubby noses are well known to the highland minorities of Vietnam and Laos and are called by many names, including *nguoi rung,* which means "forest people." The *nguoi rung* have been known to occasionally kill or kidnap humans and take them back to their caves. Many reports of this wildman come from the "three borders" region where Vietnam, Cambodia, and Laos converge. During the Vietnam War both Australian and American soldiers reported seeing large hairy beings in the country.

Professor Helmut Loofs-Wissowa, a visiting fellow in the faculty of Asian Studies at the Australian National University, thinks that some forms of *nguoi rung* may be remnant of an early human population. He calls the wildman *Homo ferus* and believes it is a form of Neandertal, but the physical description and ease of capture suggests an Erectus Hominid instead.

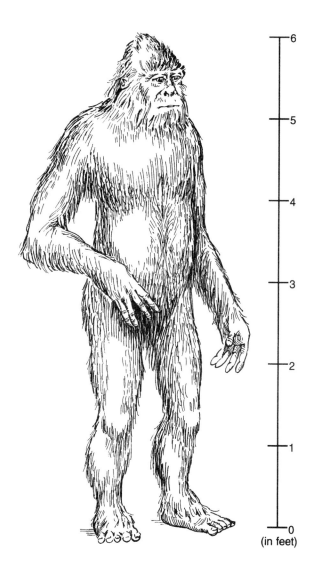

6

5

4

3

2

1

0
(in feet)

123

REGION: *Asia*	DESCRIPTIVE INCIDENT:
CLASS: *Erectus Hominid*	DATE: *December 25, 1953*
TYPE: *Sakai, Devil Sakai, Stinking Ones*	LOCATION: *Trolak Reserve, Perak, Malaysia*
DISTINGUISHING CHARACTERISTIC: *mustache on females*	WITNESSES: *Wong Yee Moi, Corporal Talib, Appaisamy*

Wong Yee Moi, a young Chinese girl, was tapping a rubber tree when she felt a hand on her shoulder. When she turned around, she beheld a foul-smelling female covered with hair and wearing a bark loincloth. Her skin was white and she had long black hair on her head and a mustache. When the creature grinned and displayed her long fangs (or were they merely large front incisors?), the witness ran back to the estate compound. On her way she noticed there were two other similar creatures standing under some trees by the river. Both were males whose mustaches hung down to their waists.

The owner of the estate, a Scot named G. M. Browne, immediately called the local security forces, who dispatched a posse of Malaysian Security Guards led by Corporal Talib. When the posse reached the river they spotted the three hairy creatures and prepared to fire on them. But the creatures dove into the water, swam under water, and emerged on the far bank where they vanished into the jungle.

The next day on the same estate a Hindu Indian worker named Appaisamy was grabbed by a pair of hairy arms while tapping rubber. Terrified, the worker ran off but fainted on the way back to the compound. When he came to he found three hairy creatures laughing at him. Later that day a patrol of Talib's guard spotted the creatures by the river again.

Much speculation by a variety of "experts" followed these reports. Some thought the creatures were actually AWOL Japanese soldiers, or primitive humans trying to get away from British aerial bombing, or descendants of a race of hairy aborigines who, according to legend, once roamed the forests of northern Malaysia. Whatever they were, they were known about throughout peninsular Malaysia long before this incident. Both locals and government authorities were apparently quite familiar with the "Stinking Ones," as they are also known. Some had been seen pulling out tapioca roots and eating them. Reports suggest they have raided crops in various part of country.

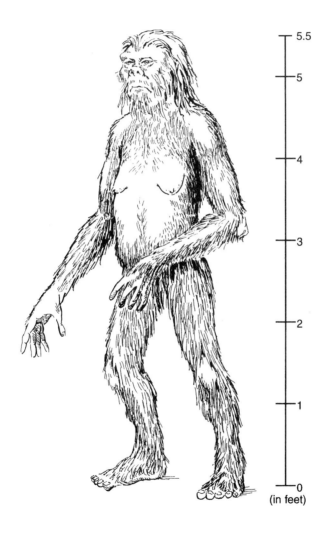

5.5

5

4

3

2

1

0
(in feet)

125

REGION: *Asia*
CLASS: *Proto-Pygmy*
TYPE: *Teh-lma, pyar-them, Little Yeti*
DISTINGUISHING CHARACTERISTIC:
pointed head

DESCRIPTIVE INCIDENT:
DATE: *April 1958*
LOCATION: *Chhoyang River Valley, Nepal*
WITNESSES: *Da Temba and others*

During the 1958 Slick-Johnson Nepal Snowman Expedition, Sherpa Da Temba and Gerald Russell, the American naturalist who helped capture the first giant panda in 1936, were told by local people that if they camped under the waterfall on the Chhoyang River, they would be able to gather evidence of a little Yeti called the *teh-lma,* or "manlike being," which regularly visited the area. After ten days of seeing nothing but porcupines and monkeys, a man told them that a *teh-lma* was visiting the stream at night to hunt for frogs. An hour later, another man called to say that he, too, had seen a frog-hunting *teh-lma* the night before.

The next night, Da Temba and this other man patrolled the stream for an hour at the critical frog time. They were about to return to camp when they noticed a wet footprint on a stone. Then they saw a *teh-lma* in their torchlight 10 yards away. It was about 4.5 feet tall, with hunched shoulders and a very pointed head that sloped rapidly back from the forehead. It was covered with thick reddish gray hair. When the *teh-lma* took a step toward them, they ran away and spent the night in a small settlement nearby.

No one saw anything on the following nights, though on a couple of mornings they did find tracks of the *teh-lma* in the gravel by the stream. The hunt for the *teh-lma,* using frogs as lures, continued throughout April, May, and early June, but all the searchers ever came up with were some 4-inch tracks near a half-eaten frog.

During the *Daily Mail* Expedition of 1954, Gerald Russell had examined some alleged droppings of the *teh-lma* and come to the conclusion that this frog-eating kind of Yeti lived in the more tropical valleys of Nepal. Other Abominable Snowman hunters, like Sir Edmund Hillary, have noted that in Bhutan, Sikkim, and southeastern Tibet these small Yeti are called *pyar-them.* The *teh-lma* appear to be akin to but different from the other Asian Proto-Pygmies such as the probably extinct *nittaewo.* The biologist Ivan T. Sanderson called the Little Yeti "the least known and the most neglected by everyone."

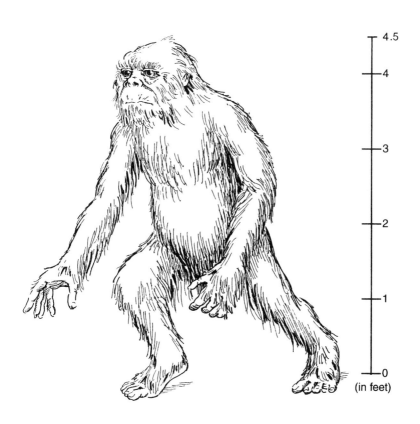

4.5

4

3

2

1

0
(in feet)

127

REGION: *Asia*	DESCRIPTIVE INCIDENT:
CLASS: *Proto-Pygmy*	DATE: *About 1800*
TYPE: *Nittaewo*	LOCATION: *Leanama, Ceylon (now Sri*
DISTINGUISHING CHARACTERISTIC:	*Lanka)*
"ancient" faces	WITNESS: *Unnamed*

The end may already have come for the *nittaewo* of Ceylon, now Sri Lanka. According to one of the last of the Veddas of Leanama, a man named Koraleya, the *nittaewo* were pygmies who inhabited the high mountains in the southeastern part of the country. These creatures must have been very small and extremely fierce as they were seen as such even by the Veddas, who were themselves quite small and aggressive. But the bodies of the *nittaewo* were otherwise perfectly human in shape and form.

The *nittaewo* stood upright, 3 to 4 feet tall. By most accounts their legs were very hairy and their arms and clawed hands were short and strong. Some reports claim that they had a thick reddish hair over most of their bodies, while others said they were dark-skinned and hairless. In any case, they "spoke" in a birdlike twitter and slept either in caves or tree houses made of branches and leaves. They ate what they could catch with their long claws.

The Veddas and *nittaewo* were enemies, but the cunning little men didn't stand a chance in the face of the Veddas' bows and arrows. At the very end of eighteenth century, the Veddas rounded up the last of the *nittaewo,* drove them into a cave, and set a brush fire at the entrance, suffocating them all.

Though this is a fourthhand report from the British explorer Hugh Nevill, the material was decisively corroborated at the beginning of the twentieth century when another explorer, Frederick Lewis, who had never heard of Nevill's stories, was told a similar tale by several very old men, also descendant of the Veddas.

Bernard Heuvelmans is quite certain the *nittaewo*—first mentioned by Pliny in the first century—were real. But what were they? Possibilities include the orangutan, a giant gibbon, and a bear, but perhaps the *nittaewo* were true apemen. Indeed, paleoanthropological finds show that fossil hominids once inhabited a large part of Asia and may have survived until recently.

There are still rumors of hairy pygmies in other parts of southeast Asia, however. At the start of the twentieth century, reports of very small wildmen with thick reddish hair came out of Laos. Many researchers link the *nittaewo,* to the Asian *teh-lma* and Sumatra's *orang-pendek* sightings of today.

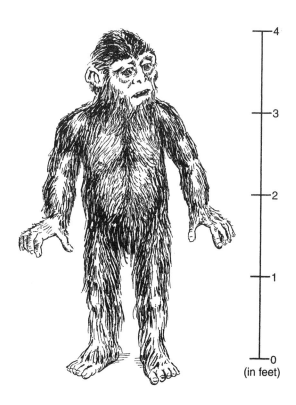

4

3

2

1

0
(in feet)

REGION: *Asia*	**DESCRIPTIVE INCIDENT:**
CLASS: *Unknown Pongid*	**DATE:** *May 14, 1976*
TYPE: *Yeren, sangui*	**LOCATION:** *Shennongjia Reserve,*
DISTINGUISHING CHARACTERISTIC:	*Hubei Province, China*
thick wavy reddish hair	**WITNESSES:** *Xiao Cai, Cheng Lian*
	Sheng, Shu Jiaguo, Ren Qiyou, Zhou
	Zhongyi

At one o'clock in the morning on May 14, 1976, a jeep carrying five members of a local forestry committee was winding its way through Shennongjia, one of China's largest forest reserves. Suddenly, right after the village of Chunshuya, a large apelike creature showed up in the jeep's headlights just ahead on the road. The driver, Xiao Cai, switched on the high beams and drove rapidly towards the animal. The frightened beast tried to escape by clambering up an embankment, but it slipped and fell into the road. The driver brought the jeep to a screeching stop to avoid hitting it. With all four limbs on the ground, the creature raised its head and stared directly at the headlights.

The occupants quickly hopped out of the jeep and tried to surround it. They approached within 6 feet but made no attempt to actually capture the animal as they had no weapons. The beast was over 6 feet tall and covered in thick red-brown hair except for a lock of purple-red wavy hair on its back. It had a fat belly and large buttocks but no tail. The fright in the creature's eyes was distinctly human, but its face was apelike, particularly its large ears and protruding monkeylike snout.

When Zhou Zhongyi of the agricultural bureau threw a rock at the creature's buttocks, the animal stood erect briefly. Then, as the officials retreated, the creature went back down on all fours, slowly lumbered down the gully, climbed the slope, and disappeared into the forest.

Chinese historical records of two thousand years ago carry accounts of these wild manlike creatures. One of the earliest dates back to the Warring States period (475–221 B.C.), when Qu Yuan penned a poem about a hairy creature call *shangui*. Qu Yuan's home was Zigui, now the area of Shennongjia in Hubei Province. Frank Poirier, an anthropologist at Ohio State University, states that these reports of the Yeren may result from observations of a heretofore unknown population of orangutans. Among the three hundred plus *yeren* sightings, there may also be reports of quite a different creature, the Neo-Giants called *gin-sung* or the "bear-man" found throughout the south-central provinces of China and into Tibet.

6.5
6
5
4
3
2
1
0
(in feet)

131

REGION: *Asia*	DESCRIPTIVE INCIDENT:
CLASS: *Unknown Pongid*	DATE: *Autumn 1972*
TYPE: *Hibagon*	LOCATION: *Hiwa, Japan*
DISTINGUISHING CHARACTERISTIC: *bristle-covered face*	WITNESSES: *Reiko Harada*

R eiko Harada, a forty-six-year-old seamstress, was walking home with her young son when the encounter began. A rustling in the underbrush drew her attention to what looked like a gorilla standing on the roadside. Its body was covered with dark hair and its face was chocolate brown.

When the beast raised its arms, as if telling her to stop, Harada went numb with fear and began shaking. Then, suddenly, she picked up her son and ran away. A hunt for the beast later that evening revealed nothing except some trampled shrubs and a lingering odor like that of a decomposing corpse.

This is one of the many reports by reliable witnesses of an apelike creature with a dreadful smell in the mountains of Japan near Hiroshima. Folklore has it that the creature is the product of a mutation from the atomic bomb dropped on that city in 1945. Because many of the sightings come from the foothills of Mt. Hiba—one of the country's few preserved wilderness areas, including Hibayama National Park— witnesses have dubbed the big hairy beast *hibagon.*

Generally reported as being about 5 feet tall, *hibagon* apparently has a snub nose and deep glaring eyes. Its face is covered with bristles and shaped somewhat like an inverted triangle. One set of footprints found was said to be 10 inches long and 6 inches wide.

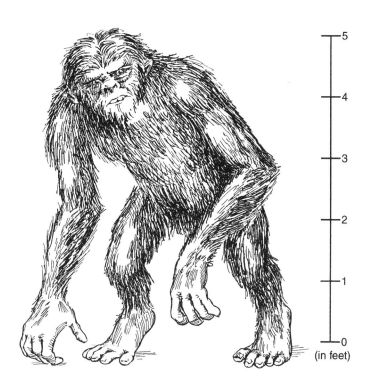

5

4

3

2

1

0
(in feet)

133

REGION: *Asia*	**DESCRIPTIVE INCIDENT:**
CLASS: *Unknown Pongid*	**DATE:** *Mid-December 1950*
TYPE: *Yeti, classic Abominable*	**LOCATION:** *Mt. Everest, Nepal*
Snowman	**WITNESSES:** *Sen Tensing and others*
DISTINGUISHING CHARACTERISTIC:	
very broad apelike feet	

After a few days at the Thyangboche monastery, Sherpa Sen Tensing, an internationally recognized Himalayan mountain-climbing guide who has worked with Sir Edmund Hillary among others, was returning home to Phortse, down the difficult trail to the Imja River, when he and his friends saw a Yeti approaching up the path. Sen Tensing quickly jumped into the snow behind a large boulder and lay quivering with fear. The Yeti approached within 25 yards in the bright moonlight, then stopped, before finally moving on back down the trail.

The Yeti was 5.5 feet tall. Half-beast, half-man, it had a tall pointed head and hairless face, but was otherwise mostly covered with reddish brown hair. It stood upright, but dropped to all fours when in a hurry. When Sen Tensing emerged from behind the rock, he saw clearly the well-defined footprints the Yeti had left behind in the snow.

Eleven months later, while exploring the route to Mt. Everest on the southwestern slopes of Menlung with English mountain climbers Eric Shipton and Michael Ward, Sen Tensing spotted a long trail of two sets of strange footprints he identified as those of the Yeti. They followed the tracks for over 2 miles until the prints disappeared into moraine. The well-known photographs of these broad, apelike tracks show the imprint of four toes together and one toe separated out to the side.

The Yeti—from the Sherpa *yet-teh,* meaning "that there thing"—is the archetypal "Abominable Snowman," known for thousands of years to the inhabitants of Tibet, Sikkim, Bhutan, Mustang, and Nepal. But the creature is really neither "abominable" nor a creature of the snows. As many researchers have pointed out, these beasts probably live in quiet retreat in the warm and steamy mountain valleys of the Himalayas, using the snowy passes as a way to move from one spot to another, leaving behind those huge mysterious footprints.

The Yeti has a conical head, stout neck, and a wide prognathous mouth with no lips. It is covered in thick red-brown fur and eats a wide variety of small animals, birds, and plants. Their feet are short, very broad with a second toe larger than the big toe, although both stick out from the others. Researchers generally agree that the classic Abominable Snowmen, the man-sized Yetis, are some form of rock-climbing ape.

5.5

5

4

3

2

1

0
(in feet)

135

REGION: *Asia*	DESCRIPTIVE INCIDENT:
CLASS: *Giant Monkey*	DATE: *June 1953*
TYPE: *Great Monkey, kra-dhan,*	LOCATION: *Gosainkund Pass, Nepal*
bekk-bok	WITNESSES: *George Moore and George*
DISTINGUISHING CHARACTERISTIC:	*K. Brooks*
tail	

Two physicians—George Moore, chief of the Public Health Division of the U.S. Operations Mission and public health adviser to the Nepalese Government, along with staff member George Brooks, an entomologist—were on foot, trekking back to Katmandu. They had moved a bit ahead of their pack-laden porters when the doctors found themselves in a thick mist at the edge of a forest at 17,000 feet. Hearing first a frightening "raucous" scream, then the sound of thrashing leaves, they clutched their .38 S&Ws and quickly scrambled to the top of a large boulder to locate the sounds.

Soon a "hideous face," according to Moore, appeared from the bushes. It had a "grayish skin, beetling black eyebrows, a mouth that seemed to extend from ear to ear and long, [and] yellowish teeth." Its "beady, *yellow* eyes" stared at them "with obvious demoniacal cunning and anger."

The creature that then emerged from the leaves was about 5 feet tall, half crouching, with black hands against a gray, thin, but well-built sinewy hairy body. Two long fangs were apparent, an the "sharp flicking movement behind it" came from its long tail.

Before the men could react, six or seven other creatures approached through the mist. One carried a baby around its neck. All the two could think to do was scare the creatures, now only 10 feet away, by firing their guns above the heads of the great monkeys. The tactic worked as the animals retreated.

The Americans thought they had encountered the "Abominable Snowmen" native to the area but the creatures' obvious tails indicate that what the men saw was something else entirely. In the plateau of Kontum, northern Indo-China, and in the neighboring territory of Jolong, the locals know of an enormous monkey that walks on its hind legs, is vicious, and attacks people. They call them *kra-dhan* and *bekk-bok,* respectively.

In passing references, the Abbé Père David, discoverer of the giant panda, noted that a giant mountain macaque (a baboonlike monkey) may exist in eastern Tibet.

5

4

3

2

1

0
(in feet)

137

REGION: *Asia*	**DESCRIPTIVE INCIDENT:**
CLASS: *Merbeing (freshwater)*	**DATE:** *November 1978*
TYPE: *Kappa, mu jimi*	**LOCATION:** *Yokosuka, Japan*
DISTINGUISHING CHARACTERISTIC:	**WITNESSES:** *Makoto Ito, Toshio*
webbed feet	*Hashimoto*

The two construction workers were fishing off a stone seawall near the U.S. Navy base in the Japanese port city of Yokosuka when they saw a *kappa*. "It came out of the water," recalled Ito. "It just popped up from beneath the surface and stood there. It was not a fish, an animal or a man. It was about three meters in height and [was] covered with thick, scaly skin like a reptile. It had a face and two large yellow eyes that seemed to be focused on us."

Kappas have been reported in Japan for centuries, being an important part of the folklore and, apparently, the real world for the locals who see them in and near the water. The traditional *kappas*—the so-called reedbed man—is described as amphibious with a monkey's head, three-toed webbed feet, three fingers, triangular eyes, long pointed ears, and a "shell" on its back. In other words, it definitely resembles a bipedal, humanlike primate. Stories of the Japanese hairy Merman, the *mu jima,* appear to be linked to traditions of the *kappa.*

Some parts of Japan promote the notion that the *kappa* are still very much around. In the tourist literature for the highland town of Tono, in the Iwate Prefecture in northern Japan, guests are told they might just see some *kappa,* described as "meddlesome water imps given to seducing maidens and eating horse livers."

3

2

1

0
(in feet)

139

OCEANIA

REGION: *Oceania*
CLASS: *True Giant*
TYPE: *Jimbra, turramulli, lo-an*
DISTINGUISHING CHARACTERISTIC:
gorilla-like face

DESCRIPTIVE INCIDENT:
DATE: *About 1960*
LOCATION: *Kalgoorlie, Western Australia*
WITNESSES: *Andy Hoad and Bret Taylor*

A ndy Hoad and Bret Taylor had just arrived at the tin hut they used in the Lake Ballard area for their weekends of prospecting when they noticed a rotting smell around the shed. Though they looked all over for a dead animal, they found none. Later, while looking for gemstones on a dried-up creek-bank, the two men felt they were being watched.

Suddenly the men heard some guttural sounds coming from a stand of scrub down the creek. When they saw dark shapes moving about the trees, they called out "Who's there?" First, a 7-foot tall female creature that looked more like a gorilla than anything else emerged. She had long breasts and dark brownish hair. Then a shorter, apparently younger female appeared, followed by a male who was easily 9 feet tall.

Once they regained their composure, Hoad and Taylor gathered up their picks and shovels and ran up the creek. But back at their tin hut stood another 10-foot-tall "hairy gorilla monster," pulling apart the walls and roof of the flimsy structure. Since the first group had not pursued them, the two hid in some scrub until the crashing sounds stopped, indicating the hut's destruction was complete, and the huge creature strode away. They then made a dash for their truck and never returned. The aborigines of Kalgoorlie later told them that this was the territory of the *jimbra*, who have inhabited the land since the Dreamtime.

These smelly 7- to 14-foot-tall hairy people with gorilla-like faces, 2-foot-long footprints with splayed big toes, and large, clearly visible genitals have been reported throughout Australia. In the Cape York peninsula in Queensland's far north, they are known as the *turramulli* giants. In the Yarra Flats regions of Victoria, the aborigines called the man-apes the *lo-an*. Sightings of the creatures and traces of their large footprints were reported by Australia's earliest white settlers and continue to the present day.

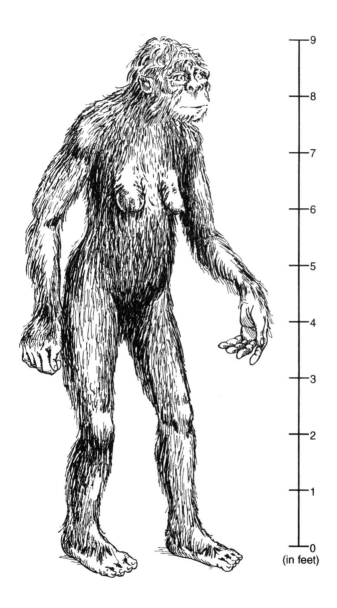

9

8

7

6

5

4

3

2

1

0
(in feet)

143

REGION: *Oceania*	**DESCRIPTIVE INCIDENT:**
CLASS: *True Giant*	**DATE:** *August 1972*
TYPE: *Tjangara, koyoreowen, yay-ho*	**LOCATION:** *Oolea Range, South Australia*
DISTINGUISHING CHARACTERISTIC: *handheld club*	**WITNESS:** *Steve Moncreif*

Aboriginal people believe that the fabled *tjangara,* or "great hairy man," still inhabits the Nullarbor Plains of the South Australian outback. So do other Australians, like Steve Moncreif, a fossil hunter. One day he was exploring a dry creek bed near Yarle Lakes on the edge of the Great Victorian Desert when he detected a bad smell. Looking up he saw a huge hairy creature observing him from a high bank.

About 20 feet away stood a creature more than 10 feet tall. In its right hand was a large stone club. They stared at each other for a moment before Moncreif picked up his geologist pick and began to back away toward his Land Rover about 100 yards away. But the creature, whose genitals clearly identified it as male, snarled, jumped down to the creek bed, and began running toward Moncreif.

With the frightening creature closing in, Moncreif turned suddenly and hurled the pick at the face of the "manimal." As the creature clutched its face in pain, Moncreif staggered to his Land Rover and drove off, never to return. Unbeknownest to the fossil hunter, encounters with the *tjangara* and footprint finds measuring up to 20 inches in length had been reported in the same area two years previously.

In 1989 a 13-foot-tall hairy giant, this time wielding a huge wooden club, was spotted by two carloads of bush-trekkers near Etadunna in South Australia. The creature, again a male, was standing on a creek bank near the roadside. By the time the observers decided to return to the spot to track down the creature, however, it had disappeared into the bush.

These giants and their huge footprints have been reported in other parts of Australia and at other times as well. According to aboriginal legend, the *koyorowen* and the *yay-ho* are tribal names for similar cannibalistic monsters that dwell on mountaintops and can turn their feet every which way to avoid being tracked.

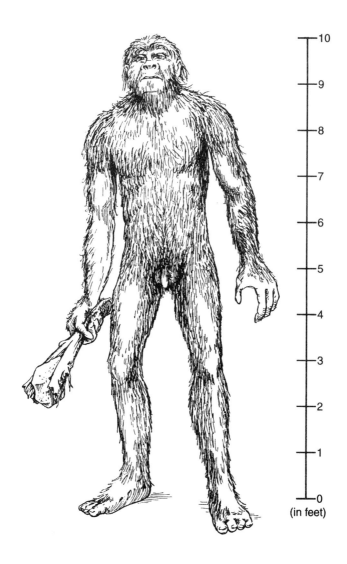

10

9

8

7

6

5

4

3

2

1

0
(in feet)

145

REGION: *Oceania*	**DESCRIPTIVE INCIDENT:**
CLASS: *Proto-Pygmy*	**DATE:** *October 1923*
TYPE: *Orang-pendek, sedapa*	**LOCATION:** *Island of Poleloe Rimau,*
DISTINGUISHING CHARACTERISTIC:	*State of Palembang, Sumatra*
very long head hair	**WITNESS:** *Van Herwaarden*

Van Herwaarden, a Dutch settler, explorer, and timber prospector, was hunting wild pig on the day of the incident. After laying in wait for an hour, he saw a slight movement in a lone tree. When he decided to investigate, he came upon a creature clinging motionless to a branch. As van Herwaarden began to climb the tree the *sedapa,* as such creatures are called locally, became plainly visible.

"The specimen," noted van Herwaarden, "was of the female sex and about five feet high. There was nothing repulsive or ugly about its face, nor was it at all ape-like. . . ." The *sedapa's* hair was lighter in front than in back. On its head, the hair was thick, dark, and shaggy and fell almost to its waist. It had a hairless brown face that tapered to a pointy, somewhat receding chin. The high forehead was underlined by dark bushy eyebrows. Its eyes were dark and very lively, like human eyes. The nose was broad with large nostrils. Though its lips were ordinary, its mouth was strikingly wide when open and showed its large canines clearly. Its ears were like little human ears, while the back of its hands were slightly hairy. The creature's arms seemed long, almost reaching its knees, but its legs were short. The *sedapa* had normal, humanlike toes.

When van Herwaarden again began climbing the tree, the little *sedapa* ran out on to a branch, which then dropped some nine feet to the ground. Van Herwaarden quickly got back to the ground and grabbed his gun. But the sight of the flowing hair from the fleeing *sedapa* prevented the seasoned hunter from firing his gun. Like so many before him, Van Herwaarden returned to Europe with a good sighting but no proof.

The natives of Sumatra have long believed in the *sedapa*—now more commonly known as the *orang-pendek,* which means "little man." The *orang-pendek* seems to have a large pot belly and may be either dark gray, dark black, yellow or tan in color. In 1945, Professor W. C. Osman Hill, a primate expert, suggested that the *orang-pendek* might be a modern, diminutive representative of *Homo erectus.* Since the late 1980s, British travel writer Deborah Martyr has led various expeditions into the Kerinci region of southwestern Sumatra. They have seen the creature and found its footprints.

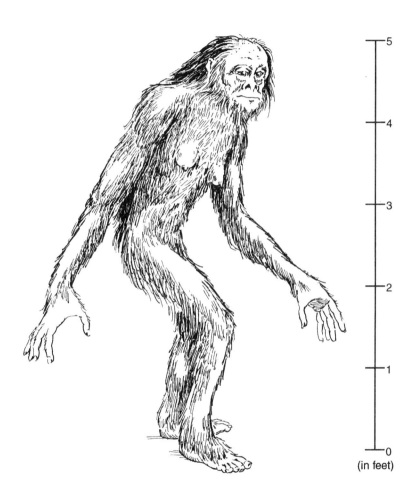

5

4

3

2

1

0
(in feet)

REGION: *Oceania*	**DESCRIPTIVE INCIDENT:**
CLASS: *Proto-Pygmy*	**DATE:** *Late 1940s*
TYPE: *Menehune, Hawaiian pixie*	**LOCATION:** *Waimea, Kauai, Hawaii*
DISTINGUISHING CHARACTERISTIC: *long eyebrows*	**WITNESSES:** *George London and forty-five children*

One day during recess, a school superintendent named George London and about forty-five children from two middle elementary level classrooms chanced upon a group of *menehune,* the so-called pixie folk of Hawaii. Details of the encounter are recounted by Reverend Kenneth W. Smith, the pastor of Waimea's Foreign Church, Christian Church, and Hawaiian Church, who had spoken with many of the witnesses firsthand, though it seems the case actually may have occurred earlier than he remembers.

The witnesses tell of seeing the *menehune* playing around the large trees on the lawn of the parish property which stands directly across the street from Waimea High School today. When the wee folk spotted the schoolkids, the *menehune* stopped jumping in and out of the trees and dove "under" the parish house, seemingly into some "entrance." The local Hawaiians still believe the *menehune* live thereabouts and folklore has it that a tunnel runs from under the parish house all the way up to the mountains.

The *menehune* are rarely seen, as they supposedly live in the forests of the mountains and normally only come to the lowlands at night. They are described as being about 2 to 3 feet tall. Their short, hairy bodies are stout, round, and quite muscular. Set in a red-skinned face are big eyes hidden by long eyebrows. A low, protruding forehead is covered with hair of unspecified color and texture. The nose is said to be short and thick.

An anthropological study of *menehune* accounts authored by Katharine Luomala and published by the Bishop Museum in 1951 held fast to the idea that there was a firm reality behind *menehune* legend and folklore. Luomala noted that 165 years previously, under the reign of Kaumualii, the last independent ruler of Kauai, a census of the population of the Wainiha Valley revealed that out of two thousand people counted by the king's agent, sixty-five were *menehune.* Luomala herself wondered if the little people might actually be a "tribe of dwarfs."

Accounts of *menehune*-like figures, "believed to be dwarfs," have also emerged from the island of Fiji, southwest of Hawaii, according to the *Fiji Times* of July 19, 1975. The six witnesses to this midafternoon encounter described seeing eight figures, 2 feet tall and covered with black hair, run behind some bushes and disappear.

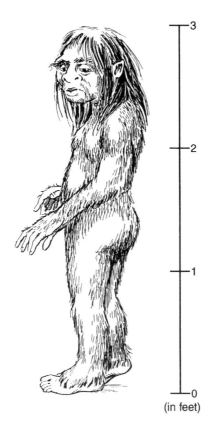

3

2

1

0
(in feet)

REGION: *Oceania*	DESCRIPTIVE INCIDENT:
CLASS: *Unknown Pongid*	DATE: *1912*
TYPE: *Yowie, yahoo*	LOCATION: *New South Wales,*
DISTINGUISHING CHARACTERISTIC:	*Australia*
long canine teeth	WITNESSES: *Charles Harper and others*

One night, Charles Harper, a surveyor from Sydney, and his companions were camping in the jungle along the Currickbilly Mountain range. Upon hearing some noises, they threw some kindling into their fire and suddenly a "huge, man-like animal" appeared in the firelight. The creature stood there barely 20 yards away for some time just "growling, grimacing, and thumping his breast with his huge hand-like paws," according to Harper's own account published in the *Sydney Sun* of November 10.

The *yowie,* as such creatures are now known in Australia, had a very small, very human face but no chin. The eyes were deeply set, large and dark, and long canine teeth protruded over a wide "horrible" mouth. The being, erect, stood almost 6 feet high. Its enormous body frame was covered with long brownish red hair. Because it was so remarkably manlike, the differences stood out for Harper. For instance, its feet had short metatarsal bones but long phalanges, no doubt providing it with good grasping power. Its arms and forepaws were very strong and covered with short hair. Harper reported that its stomach seemed to hang like a sack down its very long thighs, but perhaps these were the long breasts of the female indistinctly seen.

When Harper finally looked away he noticed that one of his companions had fainted. The creature then made off, "the first few yards erect, then at a faster gait on all fours through the low scrub." His companions, quite understandably, refused to continue the trip.

The aborigines have a long tradition of this frightening "hairy man" of the mountains, which they call by various names, including *yahoo,* a form of *yowie.* By the late nineteenth century Australia's white settlers also began reporting this formidable apelike creature and its enormously long footprint with four very long toes. The reports of four-toed True Giants have been mixed in with the apelike Unknown Pongids, both sometimes labeled *"yowie,"* unfortunately. Thus, there have been hundreds, some say thousands, of sightings of *"yowies,"* and their footprints by surveyors, rangers, backpackers and others, largely in the south and central coastal regions of New South Wales and Queensland's Gold Coast. These sightings have continued unabated into the present.

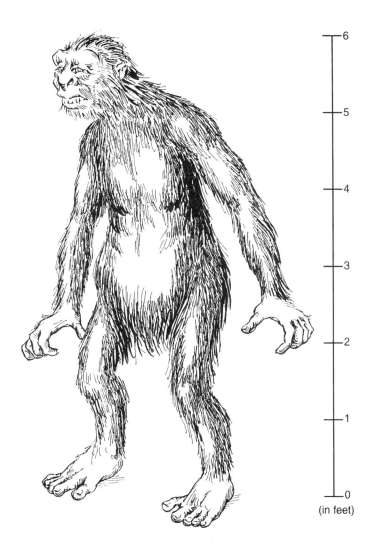

6

5

4

3

2

1

0

(in feet)

151

REGION: *Oceania*	**DESCRIPTIVE INCIDENT:**
CLASS: *Merbeing (marine)*	DATE: *During World War II*
TYPE: *Fishwoman, Mermaid*	LOCATION: *Morotai Island, Indonesia*
DISTINGUISHING CHARACTERISTIC:	WITNESS: *Rein Mellaart*
long pointed nose	

As a young man stationed with the U.S. Navy on this South Sea island, Rein Mellaart thought Mermaids were only figments of people's imagination. Then one day, he heard a commotion as some native fishermen came in dragging something in their net. At first it looked to Mellaart like a shark splashing and threshing around trying to escape. "Then as I watched," wrote Mellaart years later as a hotel owner in Penticton, British Columbia, "one minute it seemed human and the next it appeared to be about a 7 ft long shark."

When Mellaart asked the natives what it was, they replied, "We catch Mermaid again." Since it looked so much like "a real person," Mellaart shouted at them to let it go. But the natives refused. One fisherman explained, "We will not kill it. It will die itself." Mellaart then watched in horror as "they dragged it up on the sand, making sure that it was well tangled in the net. For about half an hour the fishwoman vainly tried to escape. Finally, it gave up, and began to weep like a baby." Mellaart finally ran to the mission to get help, but by the time he returned, the creature had died.

The "bottom part" of the fishwoman was "exactly like a dolphin, with a double fin on the end," Mellaart recalled. "But from the navel up, it looked as human as any person you'd meet on the street. Contrary to reports, however, it was not the beautiful siren that sailors talk about. The features were coarse, and she had a long pointed nose. But the complexion was the most beautiful you could imagine, a lovely pinky red. The fishwoman had lovely hair, just about even with the fish part. It was thick."

The local natives told Mellaart that the Merbeings traveled in schools and were terribly frightened of contact with humans. When native boats approached, the creatures would signal each other and dive to great depths. The Merbeings supposedly used their hands—each of which had what looked like four fingers and two thumbs—to drag themselves up on the beaches at night. The Morotai Islanders saw these creatures as part of their natural environment and would kill and eat them as food.

7

6

5

4

3

2

1

0
(in feet)

153

AFTERWORD

SCIENCE AND THE SASQUATCH

Few zoologists and anthropologists accept that the Sasquatch, Yeti, or other denizens of this field guide exist. Ask almost any scientist if he or she believes that these creatures might be real and most quickly will answer "no," without thinking twice about it, without examining either the reports, the folklore, the tracks, or the other random bits of evidence. Despite the fact that credible witnesses have seen these creatures, that some scientists have studied their traces, and that accounts of captures have occurred, the data is simply not sufficient to convince mainstream scientists that any of these large primates exist.

Strangely enough, even those scientists who have seen the creatures with their own eyes have been reluctant to come to terms with their observations in a scientific manner. When asked for details about his encounter with a mystery primate in Guyana in 1987 (see page 72), the mycologist Gary Samuels was initially hesitant. "I am not inclined to reveal just where I was when I saw this animal," he said, "because, to be quite truthful, I do not want anybody to kill/stuff/study/catalogue it. It is possible that I saw nothing more than a spider monkey, but I do not think so. It is not important to me whether what I saw is confirmed to be something unusual—or usual. What I saw was outside my experience and that is enough for me. I rather like the possibility that there is some living creature, some primate, that has eluded Man. I like the mystery. It is important for me to know that there is such a mystery that might never be solved."

The British zoologist John MacKinnon, world renowned for his discoveries of several new mammals in Vietnam during the 1990s, had the same initial reaction upon first discovering some tracks of the *batutut*—a shy, nocturnal Proto-Pygmy like Nepal's *teh-lma*—in the Malaysian state of Sabah in 1970. "I stopped dead," he said. "My skin crept and I felt a strong desire to head home." But MacKinnon pressed on, noting "farther ahead I saw tracks and went to examine them. . . . I found two dozen footprints in all [but] was quite happy to abandon my quest and shelter under a leaning tree-trunk waiting out a sudden rainstorm." Clearly these hominoids evoke a sense of the unbelievable that almost seems to get in the way of the basic mission of the scientist—to explore the unknown.

But there is another reason as well. Many anthropologists are no doubt cautious about unknown hominoids and skeletal remains that may be related to the subjects in our field guide because of the infamous Piltdown Man incident. In 1912 Charles Dawson "discovered" in the Piltdown quarry in Sussex, England, two skulls and some bone fragments of an apparently primitive hominid that was eventually named *Eoanthropus dawsoni*. The remains were popularized as the "missing link" and promoted for four decades by anthropologists and their textbooks as an important part of the evolutionary family tree of humans. Then in 1953 the Piltdown Man was revealed to be a hoax. A medieval skull, an unknown anthropoid's tooth, and a five hundred-year-old jaw from an orangutan were among the items used to fool some of the most important scientists of the day. Ever since then, throughout the latter half of the twentieth century in other words, anthropologists have been loath to venture far beyond the accepted knowledge of their field. "The specter of the Piltdown hoax still hovers over the field of physical anthropology," notes Mark A. Hall. "Even professional scientists can be expected to be wary of giving an endorsement to finds beyond the current expectations in their field."

But occasionally it happens. When a scientist takes the time and makes the effort to investigate these mystery creatures, his or her initial skepticism often fades. Take, for example, Frank Poirier, an anthropologist at Ohio State University. When he first examined the evidence for the Chinese *yeren* in 1983 he came away a disbeliever in the creature's existence. But a decade later, after further evaluation of *yeren* evidence during a two-month visit to China, Poirier changed his tune. "We now conclude that there *may* be some veracity to reports of the Yeren's existence," he wrote with coauthor J. Richard Greenwell in 1992. "The possible presence of one and possibly two scientifically-unknown higher primates, covered with long reddish or brownish hairs and reported for over 2,000 years, should be seriously considered by primatologists and mammologists."

Inevitably, however, harsh judgements await those scientists who wish to examine the evidence for these unknowns. This may well explain why scientists are so often reluctant to get involved in the subject. Those who do commit themselves often come out bruised in the process. The rules of academic protocol, promotion, and tenure do not allow academically connected scientists the freedom to pursue with curiosity any interest they might have in hominology or even to be cautiously involved in serious investigations of the subject.

Take Grover Krantz, for example. In the 1970s he was almost the only one in the scientific community to put his neck on the line and follow the evidence for Bigfoot. "It is Krantz's willingness to openly investigate the unknown," said Roderick Spague, a professor of anthropology at the University of Idaho, "that has cost him the respect of many colleagues as well as timely academic promotion." But Krantz was not blind to the process. "Others are scared for their reputations and their jobs," said Krantz a quarter of a century ago. "But I prefer honesty to tact."

The situation has improved somewhat since Krantz's pioneering efforts to break the academic wall on the subject twenty-five years ago. A number of visionaries in the fields of anthropology and zoology have braved the academic cold shoulder to venture into the arena of research on Yeti, *almas,* Sasquatch, and the other mystery primates. These include, but are not limited to, the anthropologist Carleton Coon; George Agogino of the University of New Mexico; W. C. Osman Hill of London University; zoologist Carl Kootman of Philadelphia's Academy of Natural Sciences; University of Idaho primatologist Jeff Meldrum; anthropologist Frank Poirier at Ohio State University; Smithsonian Institution primatologist John Napier; anthropologist Roderick Spague; University of British Columbia anthropologists Marjorie Halpin and Michael Ames; archaeologist Vladimir Markotic of the University of Calgary; Boris Porshnev, Igor Bourtsev, Marie-Jeanne Koffmann and Dmitri Bayanov, all of the Darwin Museum in Moscow; South African anatomist and anthropologist Philip V. Tobias; anthropologist Wayne Suttles of Portland State University; paleoanthropologist Eric Buffetaut; anthropologist Charles Reed of the University of Illinois-Chicago; primatologist W. Henner Fahrenbach of the Oregon Regional Primate Center; British Columbian wildlife zoologist John Bindernagel; British archaeologist Myra Shackley, anthropologist Adolph Schultz of Zurich University; anthropologist Zhou Guoxing of the Beijing Natural History Museum; Chinese anthropologist Hu Hongxing of Wuban University; anthropologist Chung-Min Chen of Ohio State University; Tran Hong Viet at the National University of Vietnam; professors Vo Guy and Le Vu Khoi from Hanoi University; Professor Hoang Xuan Chinh from the Institute of Archaeology; anthropologist Dang Nghiem Van; Professor V. Rinchen from Mongolia; and Helmut Loofs-Wissowa at the Australian National University. This truly international lot has followed in the footsteps of the American biologist Ivan T. Sanderson and the Belgian zoologist Bernard Heuvelmans.

The tide seems to be shifting. "A surprising number of hardcore anthropologists seem to be of the opinion that the matter is very worthwhile investigating," noted Myra Shackley, perhaps hopefully, in 1984. Even more important perhaps, many young anthropologists and primatologists have specifically gone into their fields of study because their initial interest in the study of humans and other primates was stimulated by Yeti or Bigfoot. And open-minded professors are beginning to teach unknown hominoid and cryptozoology courses at universities around the country, as Loren Coleman did at the University of Southern Maine, Roy Mackal at the University of Chicago, Henner Fahrenbach at Portland State University, and Tran Hong Viet at the National University of Vietnam. The University of Pennsylvania's Carleton Coon summed up the situation best when he said: "It is less costly and easier to find out what they are than it is to dig up our fossil ancestors, and possibly theirs."

Many of the scientists who have ventured forth with their

thoughts on Yeti, Bigfoot, and other mystery primates did so because of the few serious efforts that took place during the last half of the twentieth century to gather evidence of these undiscovered animals. The number of formal expeditions is small, however, because funding for such undertakings is rare. In 1954, the *Daily Mail*, a British newspaper, sponsored a Nepalese expedition of 300 people, specifically fielded to find a Yeti. It was headed by Gerald Russell, an American naturalist, Charles Stonor, a former curator of the London Zoo, and the adventurous British reporter Ralph Izzard.

Conducted more quietly, out of the limelight of publicity, were the three Yeti expeditions to the Himalayas funded by Texas millionaires Tom Slick and F. Kirk Johnson. These took place from 1957 to 1959 and were lead by Slick, Russell, and Irish hunters Peter and Bryan Byrne. At the same time, the Russians launched expeditions to search for *almas* in central Asia, the Chinese looked for *yerens* in China, and the Japanese pursued their own quest for the Yeti in Nepal. Then came the 1960 World Book Expedition mounted to debunk the Yeti; it was spearheaded by Sir Edmund Hillary, the conqueror of Mt. Everest, and Marlin Perkins, later to be host of the very popular television program "Wild Kingdom."

During the following decade, the focus of expeditions turned to North America. In California, Slick funded several efforts, often led by Peter Byrne and others, to track Bigfoot. Meanwhile, in British Columbia, Slick supported similar ventures by researchers John Green, Bob Titmus, and Rene Dahinden to find Sasquatch. But since the 1970s, most expeditions have been underfinanced and mainly personal attempts on the part of various individuals to find evidence of the hairy creatures in America.

Today, expeditions underway in China, Pakistan, and other parts of the world, are still seeking the sort of proof that science requires to accept these elusive animals as real, living beings.

ALL THE EVIDENCE

The evidence for the existence of mystery primates encompasses much more than the eyewitness accounts that many feel are the only proof of their reality. "Correct identification of an animal depends upon the nature of the encounter," noted Jonathan Kingdon in his 1997 field guide to African mammals. "In the field the great majority of clues are indirect. Most mammals are encountered indirectly, most commonly by their tracks, diggings, excreta and feeding sites." Kingdon speaks a simple truth that applies just as well to the creatures of this field guide. The tracks and other signs of our mystery hairy bipeds are found more often than the creatures themselves are actually seen. These other signs include scratch marks, handprints, excrement, hair, bits of skin, body parts, calls, odors, photographs, lean-tos, feeding sites, and rock piles allegedly made by these creatures, as well as native art, traditions, statues, paintings, and folklore— ethnographical indicators that provide important leads to the zoological reality of these animals.

Gathering the physical remains of an unknown animal is not as easy as it sounds, however. One of the most frequent questions asked concerning the supposed lack of physical evidence for Bigfoot and other unknown hairy bipeds is: why haven't any of these creatures been killed or captured? The simple answer to this question is that they have been, but few verifiable physical samples have survived the trip back from the wild. There is nothing unusual about this. A similar fate bedeviled the early attempts to secure documentation on the mountain gorilla. Even its eventual discoverer, Belgian Army captain Oskar von Beringe, almost missed his chance of proving the mountain gorilla existed. When he shot his two mountain gorillas in eastern Africa in 1902, both the animals fell into a valley. Only after great difficulty were Beringe and his companion able to recover one of the great apes and reveal their existence to the world.

Our hairy hominoids have a long history of "missed chances" as well. In 1784 *The Times* (of London) reported that a group of Lake of the Woods, Manitoba, Native Canadians captured a "huge, manlike, hair-covered creature." But no record exists of what happened to the body. In 1898, in Honduras, Edward Jonathan Hoyt killed a "five-foot creature of the ape family." But the body was not kept. In 1913, a group of Chinese hunters wounded and captured a hairy, manlike creature, known to the local Tibetans by a name meaning "snowman." The creature was held captive in Patang, Sinkiang, until it died five months later. It was described as having a black monkeylike face and being covered with silvery yellow hair several inches long. Again, no records remain of what became of the body.

And the missed chances continue. The "wild man" captured in the Caucasus in December 1941 (see page 92) was eventually killed and no one knows what happened to the body. In 1954, Colonel K. N. Rana, director of the Nepal Bureau of Mines, reported to the *Daily Mail* Expedition that Nepalese tribesmen had twice captured Yetis. One prisoner was a baby, but information had reached Rana too late for him to follow up. The other incident involved the capture of a male Yeti by tribespeople who tied it up and were journeying back with it from the mountains. But when the creature refused to eat and died, they abandoned the carcass, not realizing it would be as valuable dead as alive. Later, no one could relocate the body. The one carcass that did turn up, the Minnesota Iceman in 1968 (see page 54), was quickly replaced by a model. The case has been under a cloud of doubt ever since.

There are also numerous reports that Bigfoot and its kin have been shot and killed. Researcher John Green reports that at least five Sasquatches have reportedly been killed in North America, anthropologist Grover Krantz mentions another case, and former hunter Peter Byrne once investigated stories of a dead Bigfoot in British Columbia. However, all reports have been extremely vague and no body has ever been produced. In Mongolia two Wildmen were reportedly shot by a patrol during the border skirmishes between the Russians and the Japanese in 1939. Again, the bodies vanished.

But surely if these creatures exist many more bodies would be produced by natural death. So why haven't we found *these* bodies? When asked that question about the Sasquatch, Grover Krantz counters, "How many dead bodies of bears have you found in the woods?" Krantz notes that if there are about one hundred bears for every one Sasquatch in North America, and we so rarely find bear bones, let alone a bear carcass, how can we be expected to find a dead Sasquatch?

The problem is similar for fossil finds. First of all, no one will look for such fossils, if the creatures involved are not thought to exist in the first place. But even for recognized primates, fossil finds are usually meager, at best. With *Gigantopithecus,* for example, only four mandibles and about a thousand teeth have been found in Asia. And some of these *Gigantopithecus* fossils were not even found in the field but taken from the cupboards of Chinese chemists' shops in Hong Kong and China. While there exist cultural reasons for such bones to be gathered and saved in China— many Far Eastern cultures use "dragon bones" for medicinal purposes—no such similar practice exists in America. Besides, fossils in North America are rare in general, as the glaciers that covered large parts of the continent long ago destroyed such evidence. Of course, tropical climates are not much better at preserving fossils; there are no known fossils of gorillas or gorilla ancestors, for example. The few fossils and giant bones and skulls that *have* been found "appear to slip through our fingers," notes Mark A. Hall. They are either lost in transfer, misplaced in museums, thrown into lakes, made to disappear, or just discredited before being rigorously examined.

Nevertheless some scraps of physical evidence from mystery primates have been found and remain labeled "unknown." These include some clumps of hair from China, Tibet, Nepal, and the Pacific Northwest; samples of excrement, mostly from Nepal and California; and bits of skin from the 1958 Slick-Johnson expedition into Nepal. Over the years, the analysis of this material has received but the briefest mention. For example, *yeren* hairs from China analyzed in 1976 suggested "an unknown primate." Feces of the local Ohio Bigfoot, the Grassman, apparently came from an "unknown or human-type digestive tract." Nepalese *teh-lma* droppings contained "an unknown primate parasite" in them. Parts of the Pangboche "Yeti hand" brought out of Nepal by former professional hunter Peter Byrne and the actor Jimmy Stewart turned out, in a relatively unpublicized analysis, to come from an "unknown hominoid." Piles of droppings, bundles of hair, and bits of skin from these creatures have also been collected, but because the hairy hominids and mystery primates remain in a netherworld, scientists do not regard the mounting evidence as anything but inconclusive.

One of the strongest pieces of evidence is the thousands of miles of cumulative footprints of unknown hominoids and mystery primates that have been found worldwide over the past century or so. "The possibility of a hoax to explain all the facts," Smithsonian primatologist John Napier once noted in reference to the tracks, "is even more remote than that of the animal existing." A vast conspiracy of enormous resources would have to have been in play in some of the most out-of-the-way places in the world for all of the footprints that have been found to have been hoaxed." Tracks have been a major part of the evidence used to support the reality of these animals and, of course, directly resulted in the naming of the type now most in vogue, Bigfoot. Ichnological proofs are very difficult to fake, despite what debunkers say, because of special pressure cracks and diagnostic indicators that researchers, law enforcement personnel, and open-minded primatologists have grown to recognize over the years. Our guide book provides insights into some of these indicators for the first time.

Despite all the available evidence, however, what the public and scientists generally remember about the subject of hairy hominoids are the inevitable hoaxes, fakes, and outright mistakes.

BLUNDERS, HOAXES, AND HAIRY PEOPLE

Obviously, not everything seen and said to be a big, hairy apelike or manlike creature in the wild is a Bigfoot or one of its kin. Mistakes by strangers going into the jungles, woods, or swamps have caused all kinds of problems. We have investigated cases of upright bears carrying pigs in West Virginia and of mountain lions on their back legs in New Brunswick, which could have been interpreted as Bigfoot in other contexts.

Anthropologist Grover Krantz gives a list of candidates he

thinks could be "possible sources" for some Chinese Wildman cases that serves quite well as a list of probable misidentifications for just about any of the other mystery primates in this field guide. These include existing apes or monkeys, humans in heavy clothing, and even natural objects that have the right shape. (The unfortunate Woodridge Yeti photograph of the late 1980s turned out to be a rock next to a bush taken from some distance across a snowfield.)

Certainly the number-one culprit is bears. In a quick close encounter, some witnesses in North America or Eurasia may mistake a bear or its tracks for a Bigfoot or the footprints of some other hairy biped. But bear tracks contain claw marks, and bears, with their narrow snouts, cannot remain on their hind legs for very long. Elsewhere—in East Asia, Oceania, or Africa—foreigners to the locales of their visit may mistake a larger known primate for some huge, hairy, unknown creature. A knowledge of local wildlife by eyewitnesses is essential for their accounts to be taken seriously.

Occasionally skeptics will try to debunk a Bigfoot case from the past by pointing to abnormally hairy people or feral human beings as a solution. Is this possible? Feral adults and wild children certainly have existed and have been found. The Tenth Edition of Linnaeus's *Systema Naturae* (1758) lists seven cases of "wild children," and down through the years real historical incidents of dozens of feral people have filled the pages of psychology journals and natural histories. Deserted children raised by wolves and bears are more than folklore, but they have little to do with our survey of undiscovered primates. Misidentifications of "wild children" and "wild people" seem highly unlikely since the individuals are often dirty but not hairy, often elusive but not uncatchable. These individuals are more a matter for human psychology than primate biology. Likewise, on very rare occasions, otherwise normal humans will display a recessive gene that leads to an excessive amount of body and facial hair. These hirsute anomalies became the "bearded ladies" of former circus freak shows. But there really is no foundation to arguments about feral or hirsute people being mistaken for the hairy bipeds in this field guide.

Other than mistakes in identification, some of the evidence for mystery primates is less than satisfactory due to faking and hoaxing, and some comments must be made about these pitfalls as well. Hoaxing in this field is real. The picture of an alleged "Ameranthropoid ape" supposedly taken in South America by François de Loys was used for proto-Nazi racist promotion in the late 1920s and early 1930s, despite the fact it is most certainly a spider monkey. The 1948 encounter in the Zemu Gap of the Himalayas involving a fight between two Yetis and two individuals named Jan Frostis and Aage Thronberg is a known fabrication, yet even fifty years later it is still being touted by some as a real case. In the 1950s consultants for the Slick-Johnson Expedition were presented with "moose hairs" to see if they could tell if they were not from a Bigfoot. Other people, including some well-known names in the field, have produced fake footprints and hoax films. Fake footprints can be made from wooden feet and altered boots. One company even produced a set of oversized plastic strap-on feet that you could use to fool your friends and family. And today's digital technology makes hoaxing a film virtually a snap.

"Whenever hairy biped stories start emerging, the fakers get in on the act," said Colin Groves, an anthropologist on the board of directors of the International Society of Cryptozoology. Some hoaxes may even involve people in gorilla suits—but at their own peril. "All prospective hunters should also be cautioned that it is illegal to shoot people who walk around the forest in fur coats," remarked Grover Krantz in 1992. Putting on a gorilla suit and wandering through the woods in Bigfoot country is probably not a good idea no matter what fun you would have scaring people. Locals often carry guns and Krantz actually advises anyone who sees a Bigfoot to shoot it, because that is the only way to provide scientific proof of the creature's existence. The rumor that there is a million-dollar reward for the first real Bigfoot carcass found probably doesn't make it any safer in the woods.

To disbelievers, all sighting reports are lies, all photographs are hoaxes, all footprint tracks are fake. But not everything that is called a fake, a lie, or a hoax is one. Many people regard the

1967 Patterson film (see page 42)—without a doubt the world's most famous Bigfoot movie—as a hoax, but clearly it is not. The doubts stem mainly from reports of alleged claims by movie director John Landis that Academy Award-winning makeup artist John Chambers made the Patterson Bigfoot suit and helped shoot the film. Over the years this Chambers-Landis rumor has mushroomed into wild allegations and innuendo, but in 1997 John Chambers was interviewed for the first time by American hominoid investigator Roberta Short and the matter was finally put to rest. Chambers admitted that he simply was not capable of producing the creature on the Patterson film in 1967. "I was good," said Chambers, "but not that good." Driven by an ego that let people believe he might have been that clever, Chambers just never bothered to set the record straight.

Unfortunately the media can also be prone to debunking frenzies, regarding as fake something that was never said to be real in the first place. Take the case of the famous so-called Yeti scalp, for instance. From the early 1950s onward, Sherpa lamas and natives never said anything to anyone about these ritualized objects being anything other than religious objects "made in imitation" of the Yeti skullcap. Even back in the mid-1950s author Willy Ley was aware of the non-Yeti origin of the "caps," as he called them. So was everyone who read *The Sherpa and the Snowman,* the 1955 book by Charles Stoner, assistant curator of the London Zoological Gardens and member of the *Daily Mail* Snowman Expedition of 1954. But Edmund Hillary and the *Chicago Sun-Times* media machine behind his 1960 *World Book* Expedition in search of the Yeti decided to ignore this significant detail. They brought back the "skullcap" and "exposed" the "truth," when any Sherpa lama would have denied the cap was real in the first place. But as a consequence of this Western media game, local peoples have been seen as fakers for the past four decades. It's just not true. The skullcap was a religious object, not a biological specimen, and was never portrayed as such. "What a dreadful tale," commented anthropologist Colin Graves, upon learning of the details of the skullcap story. "To the fakers we must add the publicists."

CULTURAL TRANSFORMATIONS

And to the fakers and publicists, we must also add the mystery-mongers for even further confusing the issue. Some people would have us believe that Bigfoot are visiting us from another dimension or stepping out of UFOs to populate forests in, say, Pennsylvania. But attempts to explain one mysterious unknown with another like this are ontological dead ends that serve no useful purpose in the examination of the zoological basis for these unknown hairy hominids and undiscovered greater primates. The fact is that these creatures smell, scream, defecate, leave footprints, and are only seen in remote, usually wooded, areas. Everything about Bigfoot suggest they are living, breathing creatures that are born of, and hide out in, this world.

That's not to say that the cultural context of a sighting cannot be influenced by the roles such explanations may play in a society. When Native Americans discuss "little people," for example, they are often telling trickster tales for some ethical training of young members of their First Nation, as well as giving some hint of the biological fauna of their region. In the telling, the creature may be changed to fit the story; this does not make the creature less real, but it may change its form for the purpose of the tale. In modern Western society, the context that Bigfoot resides in, be it zoological, ufological, or popular culture, each gives a different spin on how close to "reality" the incidents under discussion are perceived or understood.

Hollywood has also had an impact on what the creatures we are talking about look like. In the fifties, with many movies on Abominable Snowmen reflecting the Himalayan expeditions and sightings mentioned in the press, encounters with any hairy unknown was a Yeti or Snowman or Abominable Snowman. With the advent and explosion of interest in Bigfoot after 1958, most news accounts and subsequent films were placed in the context of that name, even for creatures seen in Asia, Australia, and Africa. Mythic representations have shown the drift of these events—from snowy environs for the reports of supposedly all-white creatures (even though near-albinos were never reported as Yetis) to the forest-linked picture one gets of the tall, upright brown or black-haired giants of the woods, the Bigfoot of Pizza Hut. Neither has much basis in actuality; they are creative treatments of humanity, as all mythmaking is.

HIDING IN PLAIN SIGHT

One common misconception about these hairy hominoids and other mystery primates is that if they were real, they could not possibly continue to elude *Homo sapiens.* But the fact of the matter is that there are lots of places left to hide on this Earth, and oftentimes, these places are right under our noses.

The world is far less explored than modern humans commonly believe. Clusters of humans live in urbanized centers that use strips of recycled dinosaurs and ancient forests (asphalt highways) to cut through expansive stretches of unscrutinized wildernesses and green zones. Eastern Canada and northern New England, for example, are 90 percent covered by trees, and some areas of the Pacific Northwest are just as wild, if not wilder, with even fewer roads crossing through the forests. When you look at places like the Gobi Desert, home of the *almas,* or Tibet, the land of the Yetis, the percentage of underexplored territory nears 95 percent of the land surface. As a rule of thumb, the hominoids have chosen the leftover territories—the mountains, deserts, and swamps that humans have rejected as undesirable. These are their retreats. As for Merbeings, the oceans remain even more underinvestigated than any stretch of land and provide a wonderful haven for all sorts of as yet undiscovered creatures.

Another reason these hairy bipeds often seem to evade observation is that their overall numbers are so small. While the numerous names, many types, varied classes, and long history of these undiscovered primates might lead some people to think there may be one behind every tree, the truth is quite the opposite. Even where the most concentrated population of Neo-Giants likely exists, in the Pacific Northwest, the anthropologist Grover Krantz estimates a population of perhaps just two thousand, about the same as the bear population in the area. Such a figure, notes Krantz, "is well over the five hundred that often signals the beginning of difficulties due to the insufficient genetic diversity within a species. On the other hand, these numbers appear to spread very thinly over a vast area, and there may be problems in maintaining genetic contracts from one small group to another."

One result of a reduced genetic pool might be hybrids. The thought arises that some large hairy bipeds in North America might be hybrids of Neo-Giants and Marked Hominids, for example. With small breeding populations, overlapping ranges, and a reported high sexuality, the byproducts these unions could be producing such animals as the Momo of Missouri, the Big Muddy Monster of southern Illinois, and other heartland mixed breeds. A similar situation may be occurring in Eurasia with modern man and the Neandertaloids, and with the Erectus Hominids and Marked Hominids. Closer studies of hairy hominoid inbreeding will lead to a better understanding of these possible "intermediate" cases.

But to return to the subject at hand, the reason why many of these mystery primates are so good at concealing themselves may simply be because they are, like us, bright animals. These near-human primates have demonstrated a range of intelligence that may nearly match or exceed our own in some cases. "They are fellow primates," noted Carleton Coon, the famed University of Pennsylvania anthropologist, in 1978 in his only speech on unknown hairy hominids. "They are smarter than we are in the sense that they can live without modern inventions, in apparently every climate, even deserts, if the latter are within walking distance of mountains and water. . . . If we don't destroy the atmosphere, it may be they who have a better chance to survive, if it is true that the meek shall inherit the earth."

Our hairy hominoids probably remain sequestered for one simple reason: they do not wish to be found. They are *deliberately* hiding from humans, according to Mark A. Hall, John Green, Ivan T. Sanderson, and others. Some are apparently careful about leaving behind tracks and other traces. With mountain lions and snow leopards, two intelligent felines, cautious around man, why would we expect anything less from some near relatives? You can be almost on top of a mountain gorilla in the bush before becoming aware of it. Avoiding modern humans has become one of the main adaptive behaviors of all other higher primates.

Finally, these mystery primates may have *Homo sapiens* to thank for their apparent success as the Earth's secret inhabitants. Perhaps they can't be seen because our rational minds refuse to believe they exist. Sapient logic says that the thing that was just seen in the headlights of the car that looked 7 feet tall and had a white mane must have been a bear, a homeless person, or a cow. The same reasoning applies to finding the fossil ancestors of these creatures in North America. During the last century, when "Neandertaloid skulls" were discovered in the West, or in this century, when Louis Leakey found prehistoric eoliths in California, mainstream science would not allow an open discussion of the possibility of ancient man being in America before 12,500 years ago. Any notion that some evidence of Neandertaloids or Marked Hominids has been found in the fossil record in the New World is simply ignored as impossible. If one does not acknowledge what is seen, it can easily remain hidden from biological reality. For good reason, the intelligence community has long known that one of the best places to hide is in plain sight. So, too, apparently for our mystery primates.

NEW PRIMATES

A little perspective helps in considering the seemingly outrageous possibility that other hominids, other large primates, might be roaming the world's wilderness areas. First consider that since 1735, when the biologist Linnaeus established a classification system for living things, about 1.4 million animal species (most of which are insects) have been discovered and described. Despite more than two centuries worth of effort, scientists realize that most of the world's animals remain unknown. Estimates range that from 3 million to 100 million species still remain to be discovered. Primates are, of course, but a tiny fraction of the known living species and the number of large primates among them is even smaller. But even *they* manage to elude the best efforts of science to find them—and then surprise everyone when they are discovered.

Take the case of the mountain gorilla. Although the lowland gorilla *(Gorilla gorilla)* was officially recognized rather late itself, in 1847, the mountain gorilla *(Gorilla beringa)* was not discovered until the twentieth century—despite the many expeditions to Africa mounted by universities, zoos, and museums specifically to kill or capture gorillas. Indeed, not until 1861 were the first native accounts collected of a monster ape *(ngagi/ngila)* that was said to live on the misty heights of the Virunga Volcanoes of eastern Africa. Westerners refused to believe these "absurd legends." Then in 1898 a trekker named Ewart Grogan found a mountain gorilla skeleton—but as in so many other tales of Bigfoot and its kin, Grogan failed to bring the skeleton out of the mountains. Finally, in October 1902, Captain von Beringe and his companion killed two gorillas on the Virungas' Mount Sabinio. Their physical proof of the many seemingly unbelievable stories of an unknown giant ape finally served to verify the existence of the mountain gorilla. (By the way, the massive mountain gorilla with its rich black crown of head hair is easy to differentiate from the lowland gorilla, whose cap of hair is clearly red.)

It should be noted that the Pacific Northwest's Bigfoot did not enter public consciousness until 1958, almost a century after tales of the mountain gorilla began coming out of Africa. So it is perhaps rash to have thought that any quick discoveries of these American animals would occur within this century, especially considering the lack of zoologically sanctioned collection expeditions for Bigfoot.

In addition to the mountain gorilla, two other apes, close relatives of humans and the hominoids described in this field guide, have been discovered in this century. One, the dwarf siamang *(Hylobates klossi)*, is an ape with uncertain affinities to both the siamangs and gibbons. It was found on South Pagi, a small island off Sumatra, in 1903. The other ape is the bonobo. In 1929, after looking through old Congo Museum specimens in Belgium, zoologist Ernst Schwarz officially discovered and described the fourth great ape, the pygmy chimpanzee, which is now known by its native Congolese name, bonobo. In 1933, it was given full species status and the name *Pan paniscus,* and some zoologists have since considered giving this very different anthropoid generic status as *Bonobo paniscus.* And we may not have seen the end of gorilla discoveries, either. In 1990, a previously undiscovered population of lowland gorilla subspecies was found in West Africa.

Could there still be other primates as yet undiscovered by science roaming the world's wilderness areas? Absolutely. Throughout the twentieth century new primates have continued to turn up at an astounding pace. Everything from large monkeys to small prosimians are being discovered.

In Africa, for example, just in the last decade or so, we have the golden bamboo lemur *(Hapalemur aureus)* being discovered in Madagascar in 1986, followed by the sun-tailed guenon *(Cercopithecus solatus)* in Gabon in 1988, the golden-crowned sifaka *(Propithecus tattersalli)* in Madagascar in 1989, Sclater's guenon *(Cercopithecus sclateri)* in Nigeria in 1980, and the red colobus monkey (no scientific name yet) in Nigeria in 1995. In 1996, Paul Honess found the small Rondo bushbaby or galago *(Galagoides rondoensis)* in remnant forest patches on the seaward rim of the Rondo plateau of eastern Tanzania, and the Matundu galago *(Galagoides udzungwensis)* in the low-lying secondary growth forest below the Uzungwa Mountains in the Morogoro region of Tanzania. In 1997, an Angolan monkey, the northern talapoin *(Miopithecus ogouensis)* was finally named after being described in 1969. And first described in 1997 was a new species of mouse lemur, *Microcebus ravelobensis,* discovered by Elke Zimmerman in the dry deciduous forest around Ampijoroa, Madagascar. Simon Bearder, speaking at the winter 1997 meeting of the Primate Society of Great Britain, predicted that many more nocturnal primate species would be discovered in Madagascar in the near future.

Asia has been another hotbed of primate discoveries. Two langurs were discovered in the late 1950s, the golden langur *(Trachypithecus geei)* in Assam, India, and the white-headed langur *(Trachypithecus leucocephalus)* in China. A new subspecies of leaf monkey, Wulsin's ebony leaf monkey *(Semnopithecus auratus ebenus),* and the Indochinese black langur *(Trachypithecus ebenus)* were both described by Doug Brandon-Jones in 1995, the former from a skin collected by F. R. Wulsin in 1924 during the National Geographic Central China Expedition and preserved in the National Museum of Natural History, Washington, D.C. Another big monkey, the Siberut macaque *(Macaca pagensis siberu)* was described in 1995. During 1997, Tilo Nadler described a new subspecies of odd-nosed langur, the gray douc *(Pygathrix cinereus)* from the central highlands of Vietnam. And finally, from the land of the Yeti, comes word in December 1997 of an entirely new Assamensis-type monkey found by biologist Mukesh Kumar Chalise in the Makalu-Barun hills of Nepal.

But one country in South America is the clear standout in the number of new primate discoveries of late. An average of one new monkey a year has turned up in Brazil since 1990, chronicled in large part by primatologist Anthony B. Rylands of the Departamento de Zoologia, Universidade Federal, Minas Gerais, Brazil. Among these new species are the black-faced lion tamarin *(Leontopithecus caissara)* in 1990, the zebra marmoset *(Callithrix mauesi)* in 1992, another new marmoset *(Callithrix nigriceps)* in 1992, a new monkey *(Cebus kaapori)* in 1992, another new marmoset *(Callithrix marcai)* in 1993, and yet another, the Satere marmoset *(Callithrix saterei)* in 1996, as well as the black-headed sagui dwarf monkey, as yet unnamed scientifically, in 1997. In 1997 alone the Dutch primatologist Marc van Roosemalen combed the Brazilian rain forest and found five new species of monkey, including a dwarf marmoset, the manicore marmoset, and another member of the Callicebus genus, which the locals call the *zog-zog*—probably from the sound the throaty duet couples sing to establish their territory. Still to come from van Roosemalen are descriptions of two more monkey species, not to mention the new species of tapir and jaguar he also found.

We can be sure that science will continue to find still more primates in the years and decades to come—perhaps even some of those described in this controversial volume.

BEST BETS

There are some fifty individual mystery primates portrayed in our field guide, but some were last seen centuries ago and their descendants in those places probably no longer exist today. No Proto-Pygmies, True Giants, or Marked Hominids are likely to still be stalking the wilds of Europe, for example. Reports of these creatures are old tales, ancient sightings, and archetypal memories of the days when they were more numerous in Europe. Grendel is an example of an important link to the past, but it has nothing to do with the current range of True Giants. It is possible that some interlopers, mainly the more common Marked Hominids, could occasionally make tracks into Lapland, Germany's Black Forest, or the Alps, but these would be rare events.

Tales of giants and little people in general also seem rather unlikely, but a few "hot spots" of current sightings, footprint finds, and hair and fecal evidence, do exist. Just as elusive are the Merbeings. Though they may have overrun the planet—in oceans, lakes, rivers, and coastal lands—at one time, what we are seeing today are probably remnants of a success long passed. Chances of catching such a creature are admittedly quite slim. So the question naturally arises: which of this field guide's unknown hairy hominoids are most likely to be discovered in the next century?

We believe that the most likely candidate is the *orang-pendek*. These Proto-Pygmies are getting a great deal of attention since Flora and Fauna International, a conservation group based in the United Kingdom, began sponsoring successive expeditions to Sumatra. Field leader Debbie Martyr, plus British photographer Jeremy Holden and Indonesian anthropologist Yanuar Achmad, claim they have found footprints and actually seen an *orang-pendek* as it roamed the slopes of Mount Kerinci, a 13,000-foot peak deep in the region's national park. Of all the unknown hairy biped research efforts, this one is the most likely to produce positive results the soonest. But, it should be noted, the researchers are worried that after all the recent droughts and forest fires there may no longer be a sustainable population of *orang-pendek* in Sumatra. "Are we wiping out species before we even know, formally, that they exist?" asks Debbie Martyr.

Our next best bet is the Pacific Northwest's Bigfoot/Sasquatch. The great number of Americans and Canadians searching for these Neo-Giants make the odds high for some type of discovery. Ray Crowe's Western Bigfoot Society, Cliff Crook's Bigfoot Central, Robert Morgan's American Anthropological Research Foundation, and Tod Deery's North American Science Institute all are lending some support to the quest. Nevertheless, the first Bigfoot may be obtained, by accident, when hit by a lumber truck or some other chance happening. Or Grover Krantz might shoot one.

Another highly promising candidate for discovery is the *nguoi rung*. Due to the exciting work of zoologist John MacKinnon, who is funded by the Vietnamese government and the World Wildlife Fund, the Vu Quang forest reserve in Vietnam, where many new major animal discoveries have been made recently, seems a likely spot for new larger primate finds as well. Vietnamese scientists Tran Hong Viet and Dang Nghiem Van, among others, have focused on the three-borders region where Vietnam, Cambodia, and Laos converge, as the center of their searches for the Vietnamese Wildman, the *nguoi rung*.

Less likely than our first three candidates but still a very good bet is the *yeren*. Recently, the focus has been on China, where scientists are taking seriously a spate of Wildman reports and claim to have obtained hair samples that prove the existence of the creatures. News of expeditions throughout the 1990s demonstrate that the Chinese are unflinching in their efforts to find their Wildmen or *yerens*. In 1995, for example, they sent a thirty-member team into central China's Shennongjia Nature Reserve—a known area for rare animals, including the golden monkey, as well as a hot spot for *yeren* sightings, footprint finds, and the occasional hair sample. Anthropologists, biologists, and geneticists from the Chinese Academy of Science, prestigious Beijing University, and Beijing Normal University participated in the effort. And more new field studies were conducted in 1996 and 1997. China may hold the key to finding an unknown hairy hominid merely by putting the most teams in the field regularly.

Another promising candidate is the *almas* of the Caucasus. Over a span of four decades, the former Soviet Union backed searches for the *almas* of the Caucasus mountains east of the Black Sea. While the current Russian economy does not lend itself to such ventures, there is a good chance the search will continue with funding from other sources. Much hope rests on the shoulders of Marie-Jeanne Koffmann, the remarkable seventy-nine-year-old French-born Russian, who, after an adventurous career in the Red Army, spent over twenty years traveling the mountains on horseback to interview an estimated five hundred eyewitnesses, collecting unidentified footprints, and examining piles of suspected *almas* droppings. Koffmann, who recently retired on a small pension and returned to France, summarized her findings in two articles published in the journal *Archeologia* in 1991. These articles drew the attention of a documentary filmmaker named Sylvain Pallix, who managed not only to bring Koffmann out of retirement, but to raise the finances to support a Franco-Russian expedition, complete with ten scientists and a documentary film crew. Though their 1992 expedition did not capture a live *almas* on film or bring back any new biological samples, interest in these creatures remains high and Koffmann continues to write up her fieldwork findings in *Archeologia*. Others will search for these animals in the coming years; Robert Morgan, for example, will be leading an expedition to Mongolia.

At least as well attested as the Caucasus folklore on the *almas* collected by Koffmann are the Pamirs' Wildman or *kaptar* traditions from Central Asia, our next best bet. The area has been the subject of several significant but neglected and underpublicized Russian expeditions. During the cold war, the Russian Snowman Commission and the later Relict Hominoid Research Seminar were in the forefront of the known efforts. Now passionate renewed efforts are coming from Russia through Dmitri Bayanov, Igor Bourtsev, Vadim Makarov, and others at the Darwin Museum, and biologist Valentin B. Sapunov in St. Petersburg. Interest in pursuing hominid surveys in the Pamirs, with an eye toward collecting more footprint samples and film of these animals, appears to be on the minds of many Russian scholars. In October 1997, Moscow hosted an international conference on unknown hominoids, and hopes are running high in Russia that they will be able to mount more expeditions in search of the *kaptar*.

Our dark horse candidate is an Erectus Hominid from northern Pakistan. From 1992 through at least May 1994, French expeditions to the Shishi Kuh valley in the Chitral region of Pakistan investigated the *barmanu* (which means the "big hairy one"), and found footprints. Dr. Anne Mallasseand, zoologist Jordi Magraner, and another associate, all Europeans, said they also had heard unusual guttural sounds that could have been made by a primitive voicebox. They then tracked down the witnesses who claimed to have seen the horrible-smelling animal that made them. According to the expedition leaders, eyewitnesses asked to choose among various images of mystery primates, most often selected pictures of the Minnesota Iceman (see page 54) to describe what they had seen. Further *barmanu* seeking expeditions into Pakistan have occurred throughout the 1990s, and plans for others appear to be in the works.

Our final best bet is the Yeti, which may have Hollywood to thank—or blame—for its discovery. A new spotlight will be focused on the Himalayas, Tibet, and Nepal during the coming years. Maybe it is a 1950s retro effect or the political connection to the heightened awareness issuing from His Holiness the Dalai Lama, but a rash of new movies will bring this Unknown Pongid, the classic Abominable Snowman, back into the public spotlight. The films include the Nicolas Cage/20th Century Fox's *Tom Slick: Monster Hunter,* Warner Brs./George Clooney Production Company's *The Long Walk,* and Jean-Claude Van Damme's *Abominable.* The renewed popularity of the Yeti will likely secure new funding for expeditions that, with luck, may yield some evidence of that most famous of mystery primates from the roof of the world.

IF YOU SHOULD SEE ONE . . .

So what should you do if you see a Bigfoot, Yeti, *almas, yeren,* or any one of the other types mentioned in this field guide? There are two major approaches to this issue. One approach, originally suggested by Tom Slick, and now led by Grover Krantz, John Green, and Daniel Perez, acknowledges that these creatures will not be scientifically accepted until there is a corpse. Krantz is very specific about what to do after you kill one: "The best procedure is to cut off the biggest piece you can carry and then go for help to retrieve the remainder."

The other approach, a decidedly nonviolent one, was first promoted by the late hominoid newsletter editor George Haas and is now led by Peter Byrne who, after years of being a big-game hunter and killing many trophy elephants and tigers in Asia, feels that photography is the answer to proving the animals exist. Rene Dahinden and Robert W. Morgan are other leading exponents of the "no kill" school. Videotaping, live capture, or tranquilizing the animal and taking biological samples all fit within this nonviolent approach. Mark A. Hall calls this *telebiology,* "using our brains and our technology" to study these creatures "at a distance."

Of course, most people coming face to face with a hairy hominid or mystery primate will be surprised by their encounter and will probably not have either a gun or a camera on hand. The best you can do, under such circumstances, is note the location, make a quick drawing of what you saw, take plaster casts of any available footprints, and notify an interested hominoid researcher in your area. (See the list of available resources at the end of this field guide.) Of course, don't expect anyone to believe you.

No one really knows when, or if, these creatures will ever be accepted by science. Certainly the legwork has been done. The reports have been gathered and correlated. And the theories have been proposed. So what's left? The only thing that can really make a difference now is an observation that cannot be ignored. In other words, what's needed, to quote Eastern Michigan University sociologist Ron Westrum, is "a lucky break."

ACKNOWLEDGMENTS

This field guide is the result of decades of research in the field and in the libraries of the world, and we appreciate the help that hundreds of people have provided in making this work a reality. Foremost among them is Mark A. Hall of Minnesota for years of intellectual stimulation, research exchanges, and classification debates, which continued through his critiques of a draft of his work. And for numerous bits of information contained in this book of a very technical nature regarding primatology and paleoanthropology, we thank the following people for passing along their insights: Noel Rowe, Colin Groves, Anthony B. Rylands, Jerzy Dyczkowski, Michel Raynal, Jeff Meldrum, Gordon Strasenburgh, Carroll Riley, George Agogino, Carleton Coon, C. Loring Brace, Eric Pettifor, Matt Bille, Dan Porter, and Phil Sirois.

A variety of materials, reports, casts, ideas, and suggestions from an international selection of hominoid researchers and cryptozoologists have led to the concepts and understandings revealed, for the first time, in the pages of this book. Words of appreciation go out to John Green, Debbie Martyr, Dmitri Bayanov, Peter Byrne, Rene Dahinden, Grover S. Krantz, Bobbie Short, Bernard Heuvelmans, Danny Perez, Scott McNabb, Ron Schaffner, Ray Crowe, Paul Cropper, Henry Franzoni, Henner Fahrenbach, Matt Moneymaker, Chris Kraska, Ira Walters, Donald Shannon, Tod Deery, Jeff Glickman, Christopher Murphy, Jim McLeod, John Kirk, Kyle Mizokami, Jerome Clark, Ira Walters, Robert Rickard, Janet Bord, Robert Stansberry, Vern Weitzel, and last, but by no means least, to the late Ivan T. Sanderson.

A final round of thanks goes to our "bookends." At one end, we have all the witnesses who have come forward, often fearlessly, with their accounts over the years—and this includes a few scientists who have been especially courageous in relating their encounters, considering the possible repercussions to their careers. And at the other end, we have literary agent Harvey Klinger and Avon editors Jennifer Brehl and Clare Hutton, who took it the final step of the way. Thank you all.

CASE SOURCES

NORTH AMERICA

BIGFOOT: Mark A. Hall, "Patterson's Bigfoot," in *The Yeti, Bigfoot & True Giants,* 2nd ed. (Minneapolis, Minn.: MAHP, 1997); Grover Krantz, "The Patterson Film," *Big Footprints* (Boulder, Colo.: Johnson, 1992); Bobbie Short, interview with Robert Gimlin, 1997.

DEVIL MONKEY: Private report filed by Ron Schaffner, 23 August 1997; personal correspondence from Mark A. Hall to Loren Coleman, 1969–1997.

LAKE WORTH MONSTER: Loren Coleman, *Mysterious America* (Boston: Faber & Faber, 1983); Jerome Clark, *Unexplained!* (Detroit, Mich.: Visible Ink, 1993); Sallie Ann Clark, *The Lake Worth Monster* (Ft. Worth, Tex.: SAC, 1969); Jim Marrs, "Police, Residents Observe but Can't Identify 'Monster,'" *Forth Worth Star-Telegram,* 11 July 1969.

MINNESOTA ICEMAN: Mark A. Hall, "Found and Lost: The Mystery of the Minnesota Iceman," *Wonders* (September 1994) 3:63–77; Bernard Heuvelmans, "Note Preliminaire sur un Specimen Conservse dans la Grace, d'une Forme Encore Inconnue d'Hominide Vivant: Homo pongoides," *Bulletin de l'Institute Royal des Sciences Naturelles de Belgique* 45, (February 1969) no. 4:1–24; Bernard Heuvelmans and Boris Porchnev, *L'Homme De Neanderthal Est Toujours Vivant* (Paris, Plon, 1974); Ivan T. Sanderson, "Preliminary Description of the External Morphology of What Appeared to Be the Fresh Corpse of a Hitherto Unknown Form of Living Hominid," *Genus* 25 249–78 (1969); Ivan T. Sanderson, "The Missing Link," *Argosy* 23–32 (May 1969).

MOMO: Loren Coleman, *Mysterious America* (Boston: Faber & Faber, 1983); Richard Crowe, "Missouri Monster," *Fate* (December 1972).

NAPE: Loren Coleman, "The Occurrence of Wild Apes in North America" in *The Sasquatch and Other Unknown Hominoids,* Vladimir Markotic and Grover Krantz (eds.) (Calgary: Western, 1984); Mark A. Hall, *The Yeti, Bigfoot & True Giants,* 2nd. ed. (Minneapolis, Minn.: MAHP 1997); (Harrisonburg, Ark.) *Modern News,* 5 February 1970.

NUK-LUK: Loren Coleman and Mark A. Hall, "From 'Atshen' to Giants in North America" in *The Sasquatch and Other Unknown Hominoids,* Vladimir Markotic and Grover Krantz (eds.), (Calgary: Western Publishers, 1984); Frank Graves, personal communication and notes to Ivan T. Sanderson, 1965; Cornelius B. Osgood, "The Ethnography of the Great Bear Lake Indians," *Bulletin 70,* Annual Report for 1931 (Ottawa: National Museum of Canada, 1932).

OLD YELLOW TOP: John Robert Colombo, *Mysterious Canada* (Toronto: Doubleday, 1988); John Green, *Sasquatch: The Apes Among Us* (Seattle, Wash.: Hancock House, 1978).

PENNSYLVANIA CREATURE: Janet and Colin Bord, *The Bigfoot Casebook* (Harrisburg, Pa.: Stackpole Books, 1982); Jan Klement, *The Creature: Personal Experiences with Bigfoot* (Pittsburgh, Pa.: Allegheny Press, 1976).

PITT LAKE GIANT: John Green, *Year of the Sasquatch* (Agassiz, British Columbia: Cheam Publishing, 1970).

SEA APE: Roy P. Mackal, *Searching for Hidden Animals* (New York: Doubleday, 1980).

THETIS LAKE MONSTER: Gwen Benwell and Arthur Waugh, *Sea Enchantress: The Tale of the Mermaid and Her Kin,* (New York: Citadel

Press, 1961) pp. 208–9; Loren Coleman, *Curious Encounters* (Boston: Faber & Faber, 1985); Loren Coleman, "On the Trail: Three Toes Are Better Than Five," *Fortean Times* 98 (May 1997); p. 44.

LATIN AMERICA

ALUX: Loren Coleman, *Curious Encounters* (Boston: Faber & Faber, 1985); Bill Mack, "Mexico's Little People," *Fate* (August 1984); "39-Inch Pygmies Reported," *Chicago Tribune,* 21 October 1970.

CHUPACABRAS: Scott Corrales, *Chupacabras and Other Mysteries* (Murfreesboro, Tenn: Greenleaf, 1997).

DIDI: Jessica Snyder, "The Makings of a Herbarium," *The New York Botanical Garden Members' Newletter* 20, no. 3 (fall 1987); e-mail correspondence from Gary Samuels to Loren Coleman and Patrick Huyghe, November 1997.

ISNASHI: Peter J. Hocking, "Large Peruvian Mammals Unknown to Zoology," *Cryptozoology* 11: 1992:38–51.

MAPINGUARY: Bernard Heuvelmans, *On the Track of Unknown Animals* (London: Kegan Paul International, 1995) pp. 388–93; Ivan T. Sanderson, *Abominable Snowmen: The Legend Comes to Life* (Philadelphia: Chilton, 1961), pp. 175–76; Pablo Saldanha Sobrinho, "Encontro em Selva," *Caca e Pesca,* Rio de Janeiro, January 1956.

NEGROES-OF-THE-WATER: Fabio Picasso, "Infrequent Types of Southern American Humanoids—Part III," *Strange Magazine* 11:19–20 (Spring-Summer 1993).

SALVAJE: Marc and Khryztian Miller, "Further Investigations into Loys's 'Ape' in Venezuela," *Cryptozoology* 10: 66–71 (1991).

UCUMAR: Janet and Colin Bord, *The Evidence for Bigfoot and Other Man-Beasts* (Wellingborough, UK: Aquarian, 1984) p. 84; Ivan T.

Sanderson, *Abominable Snowmen: The Legend Comes to Life* (Philadelphia: Chilton, 1961).

EUROPE

BIG GREY MAN: Janet and Colin Bord, *Alien Animals* (Harrisburg, Pa.: Stackpole Books, 1981); Afleck Gray, *The Big Grey Man of Ben MacDhui* (Aberdeen: Impulse Books, 1970).

GRENDEL: Daniel Cohen, *A Modern Look at Monsters* (New York: Tower, 1970); John Green, *Sasquatch: The Apes Among Us* (Seattle, Wash.: Hancock House, 1978); Ruth Shannon Odor, *Great Mysteries Bigfoot* (Mankato, Minn.: The Child's World, 1989).

KAPTAR: B. F. Porshnev and A. A. Shmakov (eds.), *Special Commission on the Problem of the Snowman,* (U.S.S.R.: Academy of Sciences, 1958–1959); Ivan T. Sanderson, *Abominable Snowmen: The Legend Comes to Life* (Philadelphia: Chilton, 1961), pp. 295–96.

MERMAN: Jerome Clark, *Unexplained!* (Detroit, Mich.: Visible Ink, 1993).

WUDEWASA: Zvonko Lovrencevic, "Creatures from the Bilogora in Northern Croatia," in *The Sasquatch and Other Unknown Hominoids,* Vladamir Markotic and Grover Krantz (edrs.) (Calgary, Alberta: Western Publishers, 1984); Ivan T. Sanderson, "The Wudewasa or Hairy Primates of Ancient Europe," *Genus* 23, no. 1–2 (1967).

AFRICA

KAKUNDAKÁRL: Charles Cordier, "Deux anthropoides inconnus marchant debout, au Congo ex-Beige," *Genus* 29, no. 1–4: 2–10 (1963); Bernard Heuvelmans, *Les Betes Humaines d'Afrique* (Paris: Plon, 1980); Bernard Heuvelmans, *On the Track of Unknown Animals* (London: Kegan Paul International, 1995).

KALANORO: Raymond Decary, *La Faune Malgache, son Role dans les Croyances et les Usages Indigènes* (Paris, 1950), pp. 203–8; Bernard

Heuvelmans, *On the Track of Unknown Animals* (London: Kegan Paul International, 1995), pp. 618–9; C. Lamberton, "Contribution à la Connaissance de la Faune Subfossile de Madagascar: Lémuriens et Ratites," *Mem. Acad. Malgache*, Tananarive, part 17, 1934 and part 27, 1939.

NANDI BEAR: Bernard Heuvelmans, *On the Track of Unknown Animals* (London: Kegan Paul International, 1995), pp. 445–494.

NGOLOKO: Mark A. Hall, *The Yeti, Bigfoot & True Giants*, 2nd ed. (Minneapolis, Minn.: MAHP, 1997); Bernard Heuvelmans, *Les Betes Humaines d'Afrique* (Paris: Plon, 1980).

TANO GIANT: Ivan T. Sanderson, *Abominable Snowmen: The Legend Comes to Life* (Philadelphia: Chilton, 1961).

ASIA

ALMAS: Dmitri Bayanov, *In the Footsteps of the Russian Snowman* (Moscow: Crypto-Logos, 1996); Myra Shackley, *Still Living? Yeti, Sasquatch and the Neanderthal Enigma* (New York: Thames and Hudson, 1983).

CHUCHUNAA: Vladimir Pushkarev, "New Testimony," *Soviet Life* (March 1979); Myra Shackley, *Still Living? Yeti, Sasquatch and the Neanderthal Enigma* (New York: Thames and Hudson, 1983).

GIN-SUNG: Mark A. Hall, *The Yeti, Bigfoot & True Giants*, 2nd, ed. (Minneapolis, Minn.: MAHP, 1997); Bernard Heuvelmans, *On the Track of Unknown Animals* (London: Kegan Paul International, 1995); Slavomir Rawicz and Ronald Downing, *The Long Walk—A Gamble for Life* (New York: Harper Brothers, 1956); Ivan T. Sanderson, *Abominable Snowmen: The Legend Comes to Life* (Philadelphia: Chilton, 1961).

GREAT MONKEY: George Moore, M.D., "I Met the Abominable Snowman," *Sports Afield*, May 1957; Ivan T. Sanderson, *Abominable Snowmen: The Legend Comes to Life* (Philadelphia: Chilton, 1961).

HIBAGON: Janet and Colin Bord, *Alien Animals* (Harrisburg, Pa.: Stackpole Books, 1981), pp. 179–80.

KAPPA: Fabio Picasso, "Infrequent Types of South American Humanoids—Part I," *Strange Magazine* 8:22 (Fall 1991).

MECHENY: Maya Bykova, "Report by Maya Bykova," in *In the Footsteps of the Russian Snowman,* Dmitri Bayanov (ed.) (Moscow: Crypto-Logos, 1996).

NITTAEWO: Bernard Heuvelmans, *On the Track of Unknown Animals* (London: Kegan Paul International, 1995); W. C. Osman Hill, "Nittaewo, an Unsolved Problem of Ceylon," *Loris* 4:251–62 (1945).

NGUOL RUNG: Helmut Loofs-Wissowa, "Seeing Is Believing, or Is It? How Scientific Is 'Wildman' Research?" *ANU Reporter* 27, no. 12: 4 (17 July 1996); Steve Wilson, "On the Trail of the Ape Man," *Sunday Herald Sun,* 17 March 1996, p. 31; Nguoi Rung, Vietnamese Forest People, <http://coombs.anu.edu.au/~vern/wildman.html>.

NYALMO: Mark A. Hall, *The Yeti, Bigfoot & True Giants,* 2nd ed. (Minneapolis, Minn.: MAHP, 1997); Bernard Heuvelmans, *On the Track of Unknown Animals* (London: Kegan Paul International, 1995).

SAKAL: Ivan T. Sanderson, *Abominable Snowmen: The Legend Comes to Life* (Philadelphia: Chilton, 1961).

TEH-LMA: Peter Byrne, "The Search for the Abominable Snowman," *New York Journal-American,* 27 April–15 June 1958 dispatches; Loren Coleman, *Tom Slick and the Search for the Yeti* (Boston: Faber & Faber, 1989); Sir Edmund Hillary and Desmond Doig, *High in the Thin Cold Air* (Garden City, N.Y.: Doubleday, 1962), pp. 117–18; Gerald Russell, *"Report on the 1958 Slick-*

Johnson Nepal Snowman Expedition," unpublished document, 27
June 1958.

WILDMAN: Editors, *China's Yetis and Other Monsters* (Beijing: China
Reconstructs Press, 1988).

YEREN: Zhou Guoxing, "The Status of Wildman Research in
China," *Cryptozoology* 1:13–23 (1982); Frank E. Poirier, "Golden
Monkeys, Macaques and Wildman," *Cryptozoology* 2: 157–59
(1983); Frank E. Poirier, "The Evidence for Wildman in Hubei
Province, People's Republic of China," *Cryptozoology* 2: 25–39
(1983).

YETI: Loren Coleman, *Tom Slick and the Search for the Yeti* (Boston:
Faber & Faber, 1989); Bernard Heuvelmans, *On the Track of Un-
known Animals* (London: Kegan Paul International, 1995); Sir
Edmund Hillary, *Nothing Venture, Nothing Win* (New York: Cow-
ard, McCann & Geoghegan, 1975); Ivan T. Sanderson, *Abominable
Snowmen: The Legend Comes to Life* (Philadelphia: Chilton, 1961);
Eric Shipton, "A Mystery of Everest: Footprints of the Abomina-
ble Snowman," *The Times,* London, 6 December 1951.

OCEANIA

FISHWOMAN: Rein Mellaart, "Mermaids," in *I Saw Ogopogo!* William
Marks (ed.) (British Columbia: Special Collection of Peachland-
Okanagan Review, 1971), pp. 18–20.

JIMBRA: Rex Gilroy, *Mysterious Australia* (Mapleton, Queensland:
Nexus, 1995); Tony Healy and Paul Cropper, *Out of the Shadows:
Mystery Animals of Australia* (Chippendale, Australia: Ironbark-
Pan Macmillan, 1994).

MENEHUNE: Janet Bord, *Fairies* (New York: Carroll & Graf, 1997);
Loren Coleman, "The Menehune: Little People of the Pacific,"
Fate (July 1989); Katharine Luomala, *The Menehune of Polynesia*

and Other Mythical People of Oceania (Honolulu: Bishop Museum, 1951).

ORANG-PENDEK: Deborah Martyr, "An Investigation of the Orang-Pendek, the 'Short Man' of Sumatra," *Cryptozoology* 9: 57–65 (1990); Van Herwaarden, "Een Ontmoeting met een Aap-mensch," *Tropical Naturalist,* Weltevreden, 13:103–6 (1924).

TJANGARA: Rex Gilroy, *Mysterious Australia* (Mapleton, Queensland, Nexus, 1995); Tony Healy and Paul Cropper, *Out of the Shadows: Mystery Animals of Australia* (Chippendale, Australia: Ironbark/Pan Macmillan, 1994).

YOWIE: Janet and Colin Bord, *Alien Animals* (Harrisburg, Pa.: Stackpole Books, 1981); Tony Healy and Paul Cropper, *Out of the Shadows: Mystery Animals of Australia* (Chippendale, Australia: Ironbark/Pan Macmillan, 1994).

BIBLIOGRAPHY

Alterman, L., and Freed, B. Z. "Description and survey of three Nycticebus species in Bolikhamxay Province, Laos." *Primate Eye* (63):16 (abstract), 1997.

Bartholomew, Paul, Robert Bartholomew, William Brann, and Bruce Hallenbeck. *Monsters of the Northwoods.* Utica, N.Y.: North Country Books, 1992.

Berry, Rick. *Bigfoot on the East Coast.* Stuarts Draft, Va.: Campbell Center, 1993.

Bayanov, Dmitri. *In the Footsteps of the Russian Snowman.* Moscow: Crypto-Logos Books, 1996.

Bayanov, Dmitri. *America's Bigfoot: Fact, Not Fiction—U.S. Evidence Verified in Russia.* Moscow: Crypto-Logos Books, 1997.

Bayanov, Dmitri, and Igor Bourtsev. "On Neanderthal vs. *Paranthropus.*" *Current Anthropology* 17, no. 2:312–18.

Bayes, M. K., Bearder, S. K., and Bruford, M. W. "Phylogenetic relationships among the prosimians: Understanding primate origins and evaluating cryptic species." *Primate Eye* (63):17–18 (abstract), 1997.

Bearder, S. K. "Redefining nocturnal diversity: Prosimian primates and other mammals." *Primate Eye* (63):17 (abstract) 1997.

Bord, Janet and Colin. *The Bigfoot Casebook.* Harrisburg, P.A.: Stackpole Books, 1982.

———. *The Evidence for Bigfoot and Other Man-Beasts.* New York: Sterling Publications, 1984.

Brandon-Jones, Doug. "A revision of the Asian pied leaf monkeys (Mammalia: Cercopithecidae; Superspecies Semnopithecus auratus), with a description of a new subspecies." *Raffles Bulletin of Zoology* 43, no. 1:3–43 (1995).

Byrne, Peter. *The Search for Bigfoot: Monster, Myth or Man?* Washington: Acropolis Books Ltd., 1975.

Cachel, Susan. "Book Review of *Wildman: Yeti, Sasquatch and the Neanderthal Enigma* [*Still Living?*]." *Cryptozoology* 4:94–98 (1985).

Chorvinsky, Mark. "The Monster Is a Man: Hairy People, Wild People, and the Bigfoot Legend." *Strange Magazine* 5:24–29, 1990.

———. "Yeti and the Cinema," in *Tom Slick and the Search for the Yeti* by Loren Coleman, Boston: Faber & Faber, 1989.

Ciochon, Russell, John Olsen, and Jamie James. *Other Origins: The Search for the Giant Ape in Human Prehistory.* New York: Bantam Books, 1990.

Ciochon, Russell, Vu The Long, R. Larick *et al.* "Dated co-occurrence of *Homo erectus* and *Gigantopithecus* from Tham Khuyen Cave, Vietnam." *Proceedings of the National Academy of Sciences* 93, no. 7:3016–20 (1996).

Clark, Jerome, and Loren Coleman. *Creatures of the Outer Edge.* New York: Warner Books, 1978.

Coleman, Loren. "Abominable Snowman Activity in the Southwest." *Bigfoot Bulletin* (April 1970).

———. "Abominable Snowmen." *Outdoor Illinois* (April 1970).

———. *Curious Encounters.* Boston: Faber & Faber, 1985.

———. *Mysterious America.* Boston: Faber & Faber, 1983.

———. "The Occurrence of Wild Apes in North America" in *The Sasquatch and Other Unknown Hominoids.* Vladimir Markotic and Grover Krantz (eds.). Calgary: Western Publishers, 1984, pp. 149–73.

———. *Tom Slick and the Search for the Yeti.* Boston: Faber & Faber, 1989.

———. "Yeti: The Abominable Snowman," and "Yeren: The Chinese Wildman," in *Man and Beast* (Volume 10 of *Quest for the Unknown*). Peter Brookesmith (ed.). London: Reader's Digest, 1993.

Coleman, Loren, and Mark A. Hall. "From 'Atshen' to Giants in North America," in *The Sasquatch and Other Unknown Hominoids.* Vladimir Markotic and Grover Krantz (ed). Calgary: Western Publishers, 1984, pp. 31–43.

Coleman, Loren, and Michel Raynal. "DeLoys' Photograph: A

Short Tale of Apes in Green Hell, Spider Monkeys, and *Amer-anthropoides loysi* as Tools of Racism." *The Anomalist,* 4:84–93 (Autumn 1996).

Coon, Carleton. "Why There Has to Be a Sasquatch," in *The Sasquatch and Other Unknown Hominoids.* Vladimir Markotic and Grover Krantz (eds.). Calgary: Western Publishers, 1984, pp. 46–51.

Crowley, Kathleen. "Tom Slick/Yeti Hand," *Unsolved Mysteries,* NBC-TV, Hollywood, February 12, 1992.

Dahinden, René, and Don Hunter. *Sasquatch/Bigfoot: The Search for North America's Incredible Creature.* Buffalo: Firefly Books, 1993.

Dao Van Tien. "Sur une nouvelle espéce de Nycticebus au Vietnam." *Zoologischer Anz.* 164:240–43 (1960).

Dong, Paul. "Wildman," in *The Four Major Mysteries of Mainland China.* Englewood Cliffs, N.J.: Prentice-Hall, (1984).

Frayer, David W. *"Gigantopithecus* and Its Relationship to *Australopithecus." American Journal of Physical Anthropoloy* 39:413–26 (1972).

Gordon, David George. *Field Guide to the Sasquatch.* Seattle, Wash.: Sasquatch Books, 1992.

Green, John. *On the Track of the Sasquatch.* Agassiz, B.C.: Cheam Publishing Ltd., 1968.

———. *Year of the Sasquatch.* Agassiz, B.C.: Cheam Publishing Ltd., 1970.

———. *The Sasquatch File.* Agassiz, B.C.: Cheam Publishing Ltd., 1970.

———. *Sasquatch: The Apes Among Us.* Seattle, Wash.: Hanover House, 1978.

Groves, Colin P. "Order Primates," in *Mammal Species of the World: A Taxonomic and Geographic Reference.* D. E. Wilson and D. M. Reeder (eds.). Washington, D.C.: Smithsonian Institution Press, 1993.

Hall, Mark A. "Contemporary Stories of 'Taku He' or 'Bigfoot' in South Dakota as Drawn from Newspaper Accounts." *The Minnesota Archaeologist* 37, no. 2:63–78 (May 1978).

———. "Encounters with True Giants, 1829–1994." *Wonders* 4:63–79 (1995).

————. "Stories of 'Bigfoot' in Iowa During 1978 as Drawn from Newspaper Sources." *The Minnesota Archaeologist* 38, no. 1:2–17 (December 1979)

————. "The Gardar Skull and the Taller-hominid." *Wonders* 4:3–10 (1995).

————."The Great Swamps." *Natural Mysteries*. Minneapolis, Minn.: MAHP, 1989.

————. "On Giant Apes Reported in Africa." Unpublished manuscript. 12 June 1972.

————. *The Yeti, Bigfoot & True Giants,* 2nd ed. Minneapolis, Minn.: MAHP, 1997.

Halpin, Marjorie, and Michael Ames (eds.). *Manlike Monsters on Trial: Early Records and Modern Evidence.* Vancouver: University of British Columbia Press, 1980.

Heuvelmans, Bernard. "Annotated Checklist of Apparently Unknown Animals with which Cryptozoology is Concerned." *Cryptozoology* 5:1–16 (1986).

————. *On the Track of Unknown Animals.* London: Kegan Paul International, 1995.

Honess, P. E. "Speciation among Galagos (Primates, Galagidae) in Tanzanian Forests." Unpublished doctoral thesis, Oxford Brookes University, Oxford, UK. 1996.

————. "Taxonomic revision of the galagos: Academic indulgence or practical necessity?" *Primate Eye* (63):21 (abstract), 1997.

Huyghe, Patrick. "Sasquatch!" *Glowing Birds: Stories from the Edge of Science.* Boston: Faber & Faber, 1985.

Izzard, Ralph. *The Abominable Snowman Adventure.* London: Hodder and Stoughton, 1955.

Johanson, Donald, and Blake Edgar. *From Lucy to Language.* New York: Simon & Schuster, 1996.

Kingdon, Jonathan. *The Kingdon Field Guide to African Mammals.* San Diego: Academic Press Natural World, 1997.

Koffmann, Marie-Jeanne. "Brief Ecological Description of the Caucasus Relic Hominoid," in *The Sasquatch and Other Unknown Hominoids.* Vladimir Markotic and Grover Krantz (eds.). Calgary: Western Publishers, 1984.

———. "L'Almasty du Caucase, mode de vie d'un hominide." *Archeologia,* 52–65 (February 1992).

———. "L'Almasty, yeti du Caucase." *Archeologia,* 24–43 (June 1991).

———. "Les hominoides reliques dans l'antiquité." *Archeologia,* 33-43 (December 1994).

———. "Les hominoides reliques dans l'antiquité." *Archeologia,* 56–66 (January 1995).

Krantz, Grover S. *Big Footprints: A Scientific Inquiry into the Reality of Sasquatch.* Boulder, Colo.: Johnson Books, 1992.

Lambert, David, and the Diagram Group. *The Field Guide to Early Man.* New York: Facts on File, 1987.

Ley, Willy. "Is There Really an Abominable Snowman?" *Maclean's,* 30:30 (April 1955).

Ley, Willy. "The Little People," "The Abominable Snowmen," *Salamanders and Other Wonders,* New York: Viking, 1955.

MacKinnon, John. *In Search of the Red Ape.* New York: Holt, Rinehart and Winston, 1974.

Malson, Lucien. *Wolf Children and the Problem of Human Nature.* New York: Monthly Review Press, 1972.

Markotic, Vladimir, and Grover S. Krantz, eds. *The Sasquatch and Other Unknown Hominoids.* Calgary: Western Publishers, 1984.

Martyr, Deborah. "An Investigation of the orang-pendek, the 'Short Man' of Sumatra." *Cryptozoology,* 9:57–65 (1990).

McNeely, Jeffrey A., and Paul Spencer Wachtel. *Soul of the Tiger.* New York: Doubleday, 1988.

Michel, John, and Robert R. M. Rickard. "In Search of Ape-Men," *Living Wonders.* London: Thames and Hudson, 1992.

Morgan, Robert W. *Bigfoot: The Ultimate Adventure.* Knoxville, Tenn.: Talisman Media Group Inc., 1996.

Murphy, Christopher, Joedy Cook, and George Clappison. *Bigfoot in Ohio: Encounters with the Grassman.* New Westminister, BC: Pyramid Publications, 1997.

Murphy, Daniel. *Bigfoot in the News.* New Westminister, BC: Progressive Research, 1995.

Nadler, T. von. "A new subspecies of douc langur, Pygathrix nemaeus cinereus ssp. nov." *Zool. Garten N.Z.* 67(4):165–76 (1997).

Napier, John. *Bigfoot: The Yeti and Sasquatch in Myth and Reality.* London: Jonathan Cape, 1972.

Odor, Ruth Shannon. *Great Mysteries—Bigfoot: Opposing Viewpoints.* Mankato, Minn.: The Child's World, 1989.

Opsasnick, Mark. *The Bigfoot Digest: A Survey of Maryland Sightings.* Riverdale, Md.: 1993.

Patterson, Roger. *Do Abominable Snowmen of America Really Exist?* Yakima, Wash.: Franklin Press, 1966.

Perez, Danny. *Bigfoot at Bluff Creek.* Santa Cruz, N.M.: Danny Perez Pub, 1994.

———. *Big Footnotes: A Comprehensive Bibliography Concerning Bigfoot, the Abominable Snowman and Related Beings.* Norwalk, Calif.: Danny Perez Pub, 1988.

Place, Marian Templeton. *Bigfoot: All Over the Country.* New York: Dodd Mead, 1978.

———. *On the Track of Bigfoot.* New York: Dodd Mead, 1974.

Poirier, Frank E., Hu Hongxing, and Chung-Min Chen. "The Evidence for Wildman in Hubei Province, People's Republic of China." *Cryptozoology,* 2:25–39 (winter 1983).

Poirier, Frank E., and J. Richard Greenwell. "Is There a Large, Unknown Primate in China? The Chinese Yeren or Wildman." *Cryptozoology,* 11:70–82 (1992).

Quest, Mike. *The Sasquatch in Minnesota.* Fargo, N.D.: Quest Publications, 1990.

Roberts, M., C. Stringer, and S. Prafitt. "A hominid tibia from Middle Pleistocene sediments at Boxgrove, U.K." *Nature,* 369:311–13 (1994).

Rylands, Anthony B., Russell A. Mittermeier, and Ernesto Rodriguez Luna. "A Species List for the New World Primates . . ." *Neotropical Primates,* 3 (suppl.): 113–64 (September 1995).

Sanderson, Ivan T. *Abominable Snowmen: The Legend Comes to Life.* Philadelphia: Chilton, 1961.

———. *The Monkey Kingdom.* Garden City, N.Y.: Hanover House, 1957.

Shackley, Myra. *Still Living? Yeti, Sasquatch and the Neanderthal Enigma.* New York: Thames and Hudson, 1983.

Short, Roberta. "Reflecting on the Patterson Film Rumors." *NASI*

News: The Journal of the North American Science Institute, 1 (1):5–8 (January 1998).

Simons, Elwyn L., and Peter C. Ettel. "Gigantopithecus." *Scientific American* (January 1970), pp. 77–85.

Singh, J. A. L., and Robert M. Zingg. *Wolf-Children and Feral Man.* Hamden, Conn: Archon Books, 1966.

Sprague, Roderick, and Grover Krantz (eds.). *The Scientist Looks at the Sasquatch.* Moscow, Idaho: The University Press of Idaho, 1977, (rev.) 1979.

Steenburg, Thomas N. *Sasquatch: Bigfoot.* Seattle, Wash.: Hancock House Pub. Ltd., 1993.

Stonor, Charles. *The Sherpa and the Snowman.* London: Hollis & Carter, 1955.

———. *Paranthropus: Once and Future Brother.* Arlington, Va.: The Print Shop, 1971.

———. "More on Neanderthal vs. *Paranthropus.*" *Current Anthropology* 20, no. 3:624–27 (1975).

Strasenburgh, Gordon R., Jr. "*Australopithecus robustus* and the Patterson-Gimlin Film," in *The Sasquatch and Other Unknown Hominoids.* Vladimir Markotic and Grover Krantz (eds.). Calgary: Western Publishers, 1984.

Stringer, Christopher, and Clive Gamble. *In Search of the Neanderthals: Solving the Puzzle of Human Origins.* London: Thames and Hudson, 1993.

Stringer, Christopher, and Robin McKie. *African Exodus: The Origins of Modern Humanity.* New York: Henry Holt, 1996.

Swisher III, C. C., W. J. Rink, S. C. Antón, H. P. Schwarcz, G. H. Curtis, A. Suprijo, and Widiasmoro. "Latest Homo erectus of Java: Potential contemporaneity with Homo sapiens in Southeast Asia." *Science* 274 (5294): 1870–4 (December 13, 1996).

Taylor-Ide, Daniel. *Something Hidden Behind the Ranges: A Himalayan Quest.* San Francisco: Mercury House, 1995.

Tattersall, Ian. *The Last Neanderthal: The Rise, Success, and Mysterious Extinction of Our Closest Human Relatives.* New York: Macmillan, 1995.

Tchernine, Odette. *In Pursuit of the Abominable Snowman.* New York: Taplinger, 1970.

————. *The Snowman and Company*. London: Robert Hale, 1961.

Von Koenigswald, G. H. R. "Gigantopithecus blacki: a giant fossil hominoid from the pleistocene of southern China." *Anthropological Papers of the American Museum of Natural History* 43:295–325 (1952).

Walsh, John Evangelist. *Unraveling Piltdown*. New York: Random House, 1996.

Weidenreich, Franz. *Apes, Giants and Man*. Chicago: University of Chicago Press, 1946.

Wendt, Herbert. *Out of Noah's Ark*. Boston: Houghton Mifflin Co., 1959.

Willoughby, David P. *All About Gorillas*. New York: A. S. Barnes and Company, 1978.

Wylie, Kenneth. *Bigfoot: A Personal Inquiry into a Phenomenon*. New York: Viking, 1980.

Zimmerman, E. "Diversity and speciation in nocturnal Malagasy lemurs: An integrative approach." *Primate Eye* (63):22 (abstract), 1997.

Zhou Guoxing. "The Status of Wildman Research in China." *Cryptozoology* 1:13–23 (1982).

RESORCES

UNITED STATES OF AMERICA

American Anthropological Research Foundation
Robert W. Morgan
Internet site: <http://cannet.com/~aarf>
e-mail: aarf@cannet.com

Bigfoot Central
P.O. Box 147
Bothell, WA 98041

Bigfoot CO-OP
Connie Cameron
14602 Montevideo Drive
Whittier, CA 90605
e-mail: ccameron@ccvax.fullerton.edu

Bigfoot Field Researcher's Organization
Matt Moneymaker
Internet site: <http://www.moneymaker.org/BFRR/index.htm>
e-mail: mmkr@cris.com

Bigfoot Study and Research Group
Tim Olsen
1198 Oasis Street
Arcata, CA 95521–4430

Center for Bigfoot Studies
Daniel Perez
10926 Milano Ave.
Norwalk, CA 90650

Loren Coleman
P.O. Box 360
Portland, ME 04112
Internet site: <http://www.agate.net/~cryptohome.html>
e-mail: LCOLEMA1@maine.rr.com

Gulf Coast BigFoot Research Organization
Bobby Hamilton
Route 1, Box 295
Warren, TX 77664
e-mail: bobby@iamerica.net

W. Henner Fahrenbach
Portland, OR
e-mail: HennerF@aol.com

Henry Franzoni
21625 Christensen Road
Sheridan, OR 97378
Internet site: <http://www.teleport.com/~caveman>
e-mail: caveman@teleport.com

Mark A. Hall
P.O. Box 3153, Butler Station
Minneapolis, MN 55403
e-mail: mark.hall.wonders@worldnet.att.net

International Society of Cryptozoology
J. Richard Greenwell
PO Box 43070
Tuscon, AZ 85733

Internet Virtual Bigfoot Conference
Internet site: <http://www.teleport.com/~caveman/ivbc.html>
e-mail: bigfoot@teleport.com, majordomo@lists.teleport.com

Don Keating
Sasquatch Researcher
PO Box 205
Newcomerstown, OH 43832
Internet site: <http://www.angelfire.com/oh/ohiobigfoot
e-mail: eobic@webtv.net

Grover Krantz
Washington State University
Department of Anthropology
Pullman, WA 99164–4910

Larry Lund
The "Sasquatch Sleuth"
4019 NE 54th Ave
Vancouver, WA 98661
e-mail: sasqsleuth@aol.com

Scott McNabb
Global Bigfoot Encyclopedia
Internet site: <http://www.planetc.com/users/bigfoot/scott.htm>
e-mail: smcnabb@planetc.com

Jeff Meldrum
Idaho State University
Campus Box 8007
Pocatello, ID 83209–8007
e-mail: meldd@fs.isu.edu

Michigan/Canadian Bigfoot Information Center
Wayne W. King
152 W. Sherman
Caro, MI 48723

Kyle Mizokami
Bigfoot Pages
Internet site: <http://www.wenet.net/~kylemi/bigfoot.html>
e-mail: kylemi@hooked.net

North American Science Institute
Deborah Wolman
209 Oak Street, Suite 202
Hood River, OR 97031
Internet Site: <http://www.nasinet.org>
e-mail: nasi@gorge.net

Ohio Bigfoot Research Group
Bruce Rutkoski
P.O. Box 665
Kent, OH 44240
e-mail: brut7320@aol.com

Ron Schaffner
PO Box 158
Milford, OH 45150
e-mail: rschaffn@tso.cin.ix.net

Bobbie Short
California Sightings List Page
Internet site: <http://www.n2.net/prey/bigfoot>
e-mail: sierra@n2.net

Western Bigfoot Society
Ray Crowe
225 NE 23rd Ave.
Hillsboro, OR 97124-7055
Internet site: <http://www.teleport.com/~caveman/
newwbs.html>
e-mail: RayCrowe@aol.com

CANADA

John A. Bindernagel
920 Second Street
Courtenay, BC
V9N 103 Canada
e-mail: johnb@island.net

British Columbia Scientific Cryptozoology Club
John Kirk
Unit #89, 6141 Willingdon Avenue
Burnaby, BC
V5H 2T9 Canada
e-mail: blackhawk@ultranet.ca

Rene Dahinden
7340 Sidaway Road
Richmond, BC
V6W 1B8 Canada

John Green
PO Box 347
Harrison, Hot Springs, BC
V0M 1K0 Canada

Institut international du palíozo-que
Yvon Leclerc
CP 61, N-D-du-Mont-Carmel, Quebec
G0X 3J0 Canda
e-mail: yvonlecl@login.net

Progressive Research
Christopher Murphy
Dept. 291–720 Sixth Street
New Westminster, BC
V3L 3C5 Canada
Internet site: <http://www.teleport.com/~progrsch>
e-mail: cmurphy@axionet.com

Sasquatch/Research
Thomas Steenburg
Unit 701-6223-31 Avenue NW
Calgary, Alberta
T3B 3X2 Canada

AUSTRALIA

Paul Cropper
P.O. Box 13
Croydon Park
Sydney, NSW 2133
Australia
e-mail: pcropper@bigpond.com

Rex Gilroy
120 Robert St.
Tamworth, NSW 2340
Australia

Tim the Yowie Man
Bigfoot/Yowie Investigator
c/o ABC Radio 2CN
GPO Box 9994
Canberra 2601
Australia
e-mail: tbull@abare.gov.au

CHINA

Zhou Guoxing
Beijing Natural History Museum
126 Tien Chiao South Street
Beijing 100050 China

FRANCE

Bernard Heuvelmans
9, Allee des Acacias
Le Vesinet 78110 France

Michel Raynal
Virtual Institute of Cryptozoology
Internet site: <http://perso.wanadoo.fr/cryptozoo/welcome.htm>
e-mail: cryptozoo@wanadoo.fr

RUSSIA

Dmitri Bayanov
Relict Hominoid Research Seminar
c/o Darwin Museum
57 Vavilova Street, Moscow 117292
Russia

VIETNAM

Australia Vietnam Science Technology Link
Vern Weitzel
Internet Site: <http://coombs.anu.edu.au/~vern/wildman.html>
e-mail: weitzel@undp.org.au

CASE INDEX
(by date)

November 1978	*Yokosuka, Japan*	*138*
1980	*Puerto Ayacucho, Venezuela*	*78*
May 31, 1985	*Roque Saenz Peña, Argentina*	*82*
1985	*Southern Equador*	*76*
Mid-1987	*Guyana*	*72*
August 16, 1987	*Western Siberia*	*114*
August 1995	*Canóvanas, Puerto Rico*	*80*
June 26, 1997	*Dunkinsville, Ohio*	*60*

➤ INVESTIGATIONS ➤
➤ EYEWITNESS ACCOUNTS ➤
➤ STRANGE AND UNUSUAL ➤

The Field Guide to Bigfoot, Yeti, and Other Mystery Primates Worldwide
by Loren Coleman and Patrick Huyghe
Illustrated by Harry Trumbore
80263-5/$12.50 US/$18.50 Can

The Field Guide to Extraterrestrials
by Patrick Huyghe
Illustrated by Harry Trumbore
78128-X/$12.50 US/$16.50 Can

➤ And Coming Soon ➤

The Field Guide to UFOs
by Dennis Stacy and Patrick Huyghe
Illustrated by Harry Trumbore

The Field Guide to Ghosts and Other Apparitions Worldwide
by Hilary Evans and Patrick Huyghe
Illustrated by Harry Trumbore